The

Christians

of Korea

The
Christians
of Korea

by SAMUEL HUGH MOFFETT

Friendship Press   NEW YORK

First Printing June 1962
Second Printing July 1962

LIBRARY OF CONGRESS CATALOG CARD NUMBER: 62-17527

To my mother
LUCIA FISH MOFFETT
"Infreta dum fluvii current . . ."

CONTENTS

1: THE FORBIDDEN LAND   11

2: KOREA'S UNCONQUERABLE CHRISTIANS   15

3: CHRISTIAN BEGINNINGS   31

     The Catholic Century, 33
     Early Protestant Effort, 34
     Co-operation, 45

4: A NATION ON THE RUN TO GOD   49

     The Great Revival, 52
     Korean Organization of the Church, 54
     The Nevius Plan, 59
     New Relationships, 61

5: PRESSURES ON THE CHURCH   66

     Japanese Persecution, 66
     Communist Pressures, 76
     Division in the South, 80
     The Church Survives, 118

CONTENTS

6: THE CHURCH IN SOCIETY   122

     The Rural Christian, 124
     The City and Its Problems, 130

7: EDUCATION AND THE INNER CITADEL   143

8: MEDICINE AND MIRACLES   155

BIBLIOGRAPHY   170

Picture Credits   175

Pictorial Story, following page 80

8

The
Christians
of Korea

I | THE FORBIDDEN LAND

Wᴇsᴛᴇʀɴᴇʀs ᴄᴀʟʟᴇᴅ ɪᴛ ᴛʜᴇ ʜᴇʀᴍɪᴛ ᴋɪɴɢᴅᴏᴍ, this spiny, S-shaped peninsula that thrusts south into the Pacific between Russian Siberia and Chinese Manchuria. Isolated and withdrawn, Korea folded her mountains about her and tried to shut out the rest of the world. At one point, it is said, Koreans even burned strips all along their coasts in an effort to discourage passing explorers from stopping on what they hoped would seem barren and uninhabited shore.

But one of the ironies of the history of our own times is that into this seclusive land there have poured more soldiers from more different countries than the Hermit Kingdom ever knew existed. Slouch-hatted Australians, Colombians and Greeks, Frenchmen, Turks, Canadians, Filipinos, Americans, even the brave soldiers of the King of Thailand, all pushed in to fight a dirty little war in a strange little country. Suddenly the whole world knew about Korea.

As United Nations soldiers drifted back home with stories of the dust and rust and death of Heartbreak Ridge or Porkchop Hill, many wondered why the Koreans had ever felt it necessary to try to keep the rest of the world out. All that most of those soldiers wanted was to leave Korea and go home. As far as the army was concerned, Korea was the end of the line.

But for others, particularly for those who knew the country back before the tanks and bombers chewed it up, Korea will always be one of the most beautiful little countries in the world. She has been called the Switzerland of Asia. Her own people, who love Korea very much, call her "the queen of ten thousand peaks and ten thousand islands and ten thousand waterfalls." Korean Christians used to say, with a twinkle in their eyes, that when God created the world in six days he must have spent the first five days creating the Diamond Mountains, and then dashed off the rest of the world on the sixth day. Nor was this jest too hard to believe. Anyone who has seen the Diamond Mountains will not soon forget them, with their gray and yellow granite peaks scraping the blue sky. Below the peaks lies the green of the pine forests, and in and among the pines nestle the gray-tiled monastery roofs, their fish bells tinkling in the breeze, and back behind the monasteries rush the clear mountain brooks. Yes, Korea is still beautiful.

More than 32 million people are tucked away in the valleys and between the mountains of the rugged peninsula, an area 525 miles long and averaging 150 miles wide. Though Korea is only about the size of Minnesota, she has ten times its population and, in number of people, ranks as the thirteenth largest country in the world.

Some 23 million of Korea's people live in South Korea,

and more than 9 million in the north, behind the Bamboo Curtain. But bear in mind that the division between north and south is imposed from without and is no more natural than to take present South Korea and cut it down the middle, east and west. The Koreans did not divide their country. They had been united for a thousand years. When one sees today what the rest of the world has done to this beautiful little country, dividing and despoiling it from the Yalu to the sea, it is hard to blame the rulers of the Hermit Kingdom for trying to resist foreign intrusion.

They were very proud of their land, those ancient kings. Korea is old—older than Japan, older than the countries of Europe, older than all the young nations of the West. What is 1962 on Western calendars is the year 4295 in Korea.

Tradition stretches Korean history back to 2333 B.C., but fixed dates are shadowy until the time of the Three Kingdoms (57 B.C. to A.D. 668). These three warring kingdoms were Koguryo, Paekche, and Silla, and the greatest of these was Silla, whose capital, Kyungju, was for a time the fourth largest city in the world.

From the fall of Silla to the twentieth century, for a thousand years, Korea was ruled by two great dynasties of kings. The Koryu kings (935-1392) worshiped the Buddha, encouraged learning and culture, and gave the world some of the loveliest pottery ever made. The Western name of the country, Korea, is taken from the name of this dynasty. The Yi dynasty (1392-1910) established Confucianism, drove the Buddhists into the hills, and fought off Manchu and Japanese invaders for five hundred years, indelibly marking the national spirit with a fierce and patriotic love of freedom.

13

"What is Korea's greatest accomplishment?" someone once asked Dr. George Paik, who was then president of Yonsei University. The Christian educator smiled and said after a moment's thought, "Why, perhaps it is simply that after four thousand years we are still Koreans."

More than a century before Gutenberg, Koreans were printing books with moveable type. They repelled Japanese invasions with armored battleships long before the battle of the Monitor and the Merrimac. They measured and recorded rainfall two centuries before the West began to do so. They heated their homes with radiant heating. Koreans built astronomical observatories of solid stone as early as the seventh century; their great bronze bells, 1,200 years old, are in size and artistic perfection probably the most beautiful ever cast; their clear, gray-green celadon pottery was the envy of all Asia; and by the eighteenth century the Korean court was so aesthetically sophisticated that it employed more than eight hundred musicians, playing silver flutes and xylophones of jade.

But the twentieth century has not been kind to Korea. In 1905 she lost her independence to the Japanese, and when she regained it in 1945 only half of the proud little peninsula was set free. In the other half, the northern half, Communist power fell hard across the land from the Yellow Sea to the Diamond Mountains along the 38th parallel.

And yet it was precisely in these years of disaster and testing that Korea produced the greatest of its heritage of treasures, more precious than silver flutes, or celadon, or xylophones of jade. Out of these hard years arose the unconquerable Christians of Korea.

2 | KOREA'S UNCONQUERABLE CHRISTIANS

Some time before the Korean armistice, an American stood near the Front watching refugees trickle in from the Communist terror in the north. He was shaking his head. "I cannot understand these Koreans," he said.

He pointed to a little group of escapees he was trying to help. They had lost everything they owned in the world, except for a bundle or two snatched up as they ran. They had made their precarious way past the Communist lines, out into the even greater danger of the mine fields between the lines. Many, of course, never made it across, but among those who came through was the shivering, ragged little cluster that the American was watching. He shook his head again. "I can't understand them. The first thing they do as they break into freedom is to squat in little circles on the hard ground. Look at them. They're organizing themselves into a church!"

There are more than six thousand Protestant churches in Free Korea. The capital city of Seoul, alone, is said to have four hundred churches. Seventy-five years ago when the first

Protestant missionaries landed in Korea they walked for miles through valley after valley in which the name of Christ had never been heard. Today the visitor driving along Korea's highways is rarely out of sight of a Christian church.

Korea is one of two countries in Asia where the largest religious grouping is Christianity. In the Philippines the predominant faith is Roman Catholic; in Korea, it is Protestant Christianity. But, don't misunderstand. Korea is not a Christian country. Far from it. Out of every one hundred Koreans passing on the street, ninety-three will not know Christ as Lord. Most Koreans will tell you they have no faith whatsoever. In the country unadmitted superstition still dominates, unorganized but powerful. The cities are a religious vacuum. "Are you a Christian?" a visitor asked General Chung Hee Park, leader of the 1961 military coup d'état. "No," answered General Park. "My father and mother were Buddhist, but I am nothing."

Korea's ministry of education reported in 1959 that the country's eight major religions (Buddhism, Christianity, Confucianism, Chundokyo, to name the four largest) numbered about 6,500,000 followers, or 28 per cent of the population. Twenty-two additional small sects have only another 107,000 followers. Most Koreans, like General Park, are nothing.

But where Koreans have organized themselves religiously, though claims and counterclaims vary widely, the followers of Jesus Christ are in the forefront not only in power and influence but also apparently in numbers as well. Some figures still show a lead for the Buddhists, but this is a carry-over from the past and is no longer true. Recent polls and surveys, though fragmentary, seem to indicate an even higher margin of Christians than the churches themselves claim. A census of Korean army draftees, for example, reports the percentage of Christians at 18 per cent, twice as high as the percentage of Buddhists. Again, a spot survey of radio owners in the Seoul area reported 38 per cent Christian, 13 per cent Buddhist, 3 per cent Confucianist, and 2 per cent Chundokyo, while 44 per cent claimed no religious affiliation.

All in all, the best estimate seems to be that Koreans are perhaps 4 per cent Confucianist, 5 per cent Buddhist, and almost 7 per cent Christian. Protestants probably comprise about 4.3 per cent of the population, and if that seems somewhat less than massive, compare it with other Asian countries. China, Japan, and Burma, for example, are all less than .5 per cent Christian; India is just barely 1 per cent; Formosa 1.6 per cent, and Indonesia 4 per cent. In other words, where 1 in 600 in China is Christian and 1 in 200 in Japan; in Korea, 1 in every 14 is a Christian.

But more important, Christian influence and leadership in the country is all out of proportion to the church's statistical share of the population. The first president of the Republic, Dr. Syngman Rhee, was a Christian, and so also was his political opponent, the man who succeeded him as head of government in the Second Republic, Dr. John Chang. Rhee was a staunch Methodist; Chang a Roman Catholic. The interim president, between the two, was a Methodist. In 1962 the presidency of the Republic was still held by a Christian. The position had been reduced in power by revolutions and coups, but a devout and ascetic Presbyterian elder, Dr. Po-Sun Yoon, maintained the dignity and integrity of the high office.

Slice into any circle of Korean society and you find Christians: the composer of the Korean national anthem, the head of the farmers' union, the minister of education, the chief of staff of the R.O.K. army, the director of the national railroads, poets, editors, housewives, doctors, and shoe-shine boys. There are Christians everywhere.

Land at Kimpo airport and across the river you can see the transmitting towers of HLKY, the Christian broadcasting station and popular radio network that is operated by Korea's National Christian Council. Enter Seoul by train, and your porter and taxi driver are as likely as not Christians, and across the street from the station the first buildings you see are those of Severance Hospital, a union institution that has been ministering in Christ's name to Korea's sick and disabled since the very beginning of Protestant missions.

"Islands of mercy in a sea of suffering," a Korean cabinet minister called the Christian hospitals. He was paying a tribute to Christian missions at a government ceremony in 1959 honoring the seventy-fifth anniversary of Protestant missions in Korea.

"The influence of the Christian faith," he said, "has penetrated every phase of Korean life and culture.

"In the field of social health and welfare, from the very beginning, Christian missionaries demonstrated to our people in practical and visible ways the love of Jesus Christ for all men and women, rich and poor, high and low alike, with no distinction. Their hospitals were islands of mercy in a sea of suffering. . . .

"In the field of education, it was such Christian schools as Yonsei, Ewha, and Soongsil that pioneered in bringing modern educational methods and standards to revitalize the ancient heritage of learning of which we Koreans are still proud. It may be said that it was the Christian church that first opened wide the gates of academic learning to Korea's women, and it is no accident that today one of the most distinguished members of the Korean delegation to the United Nations is a woman and a Protestant Christian, president of the largest women's university in the world. . . ."

The "distinguished member of the Korean delegation to the United Nations," to whom the cabinet minister referred, is Dr. Helen Kim, a woman not to be passed over lightly and a good introduction to the kind of people these unconquerable Christians of Korea are.

Helen Kim is a sixty-three year old bundle of energy. She helped to found the Korean Young Women's Christian Association; has been a vice-president of the International Missionary Council; published a newspaper; holds four doctorates; and has been a director of some thirty-seven different social and political organizations. But all this is peripheral. Helen Kim's whole life has been Ewha Women's University, the school which Methodist missionaries founded in 1886 as the first girls' school in all Korea.

Helen was one of seven children. She attended Ewha from primary school through college, then went to America for further education. At Ohio Wesleyan she became the first Korean woman ever to make Phi Beta Kappa. Her Ph.D. in education was earned from Columbia University. In 1939 she became the first Korean president of Ewha College.

When the Communist invasion struck from the north, in 1950, Ewha was still recovering from its brave struggle with

Japanese militarists during World War II. "They tried to seize the only pavilion of Korean women," says Dr. Kim, who had fought step by step against their attempt to control her school. When Japan was finally defeated, Dr. Kim promptly raised the college to university status and began to expand the campus. But then came the Communists, and suddenly Dr. Kim was a refugee on a refugee campus in Pusan, and Korea's "only pavilion of women" was nothing but a motley cluster of tents and shacks in a sea of mud. Nothing, however, was able to break Helen Kim's stubborn determination to keep her Christian school alive.

Late in 1961 Dr. Kim retired after forty-four years of service to her alma mater. Under this diminutive but indomitable president, the little Methodist school, struggling against the ingrained Korean suspicion of education for women, rocketed from a student body of 380 to more than eight thousand and became, probably, the largest women's university in the world. Hundreds have been won to Christ on its campus. Every year from five hundred to seven hundred girls accept Christ as Savior at the annual campus evangelistic services.

As for the future? "Old teachers never stop," observes Dr. Kim, "they keep moving forward." Three years ago, when she first tried to retire, this educator and diplomat, Korea's greatest living woman, said very simply, "I have been very busy and very happy here, perhaps too busy. I feel in my heart that I want more time to tell others about Jesus Christ. Now I want to give my place in the school to someone else and spend the remaining years of my life as an evangelist, speaking for Christ in the village churches."

Here is one of the secrets of the strength of the Korean

church: whatever their other callings may be, Korea's Christians are unashamed evangelists and witnesses for Christ. Helen Kim, delegate to the United Nations, university president, citizen of the world, finds her greatest joy at last in preaching to her people in country churches.

But just as the Korean church's educators are evangelists, so also are her evangelists often educators. Take Dr. Kyung-Chik Han, for example, who is as famous in Korea as Helen Kim.

Mild mannered and frail, hollowed by a long forgotten battle with tuberculosis, Dr. Han is not the kind of man who stands out in a crowd, but once you know him you never forget him. He is pastor of Seoul's great Presbyterian Church of Eternal Joy (Yung Nak), where six thousand people flock to hear him preach every Sunday, making his congregation the largest in Korea.

His ministry is a unique blend of contrasts. He preaches so that the weariest of country grandmothers can understand him, but crowds of Seoul's long-haired students hang on his every word. He gives the impression of being almost otherworldly, but he was one of the first to plunge into the political reorganization of Korea after independence in 1945. He is still at heart a country pastor, but he ministers to the largest congregation in the largest and most sophisticated city in all Korea, and he has served as president of the country's oldest Christian college.

Life really began for Kyung-Chik Han back in a tiny, thatch-roofed village of thirty-five houses in northern Korea when his second cousin, a Confucian scholar, became the first Christian in the village. Soon a little church was organized, and a primary school was started. Since his cousin was the school teacher, Han's parents entered him in the first grade at the age of seven. Ever since, church and school, side by side, ministering each in its own way for Christ, have been the consuming passions of Kyung-Chik Han's life.

High school under one of Korea's great Christian patriots, Man-Shik Cho, a leader of independence struggles against Japan, marked Han forever as a proud, free, and independent Korean; while Union Christian College (now Soongsil University) brought him into an intimate and loyal relationship with missionaries. It was a good combination. He has never been afraid to disagree with missionaries, but he has never ceased to love and admire them.

To further prepare himself, Han went to America where he studied at the College of Emporia (Kansas) and Princeton (New Jersey) Theological Seminary, earning his way by washing dishes. His alma mater, Union Christian College, called him back to Korea to its chair of Bible, but pupils of Man-Shik Cho were suspect in Japanese-occupied Korea, and the authorities blocked his appointment. So Han went instead to the far north, to a pastorate on the Yalu River. But again the Japanese interfered. Police ousted him from his pulpit, and he retired to the country, farming with his own hands the land of a combined old folks home and orphanage, of which he became the director.

When victory in the Pacific brought liberation to Korea in 1945, joy was quickly quenched by the discovery that the northern half of the country had been relinquished to the Russians. Dismayed but still hopeful, northern Koreans moved quickly to try to establish patterns for a free and democratic Korea before the Russian hand fell too heavily on the region.

In Sinuiju, where about one-fourth of the city's inhabitants were Christian, Han joined with another pastor and organized the Christian Social Democratic party to work for the freedom and social reconstruction of the country. At first the membership was all Christian, but realizing that this was too narrow a foundation for political stability, the leaders dropped the word "Christian" from the name and invited all to join for an independent and united Korea.

But the Communists had other plans. Squads of hoodlums were rushed to the area to break up meetings of the Christian political party. A leading elder was beaten to death, and the homes of the party's executive committee were attacked and damaged. Five thousand students, many of them Christians, rose up in Sinuiju to protest Communist suppression of the freedom party. They were fired upon in the streets. But by the grace of God, Kyung-Chik Han managed to escape before the demonstrations. Slipping away to the border, he hiked the last fifty miles across the line into the American zone by night, reaching Seoul in October, 1945.

"A good many young people followed me down to Seoul," says Dr. Han. "We didn't know what was happening or what was ahead of us. Everybody was lonesome, and naturally we got together for prayer meetings." Soon they were meeting for regular worship in an abandoned Japanese Shinto shrine. By spring the congregation numbered five hundred and had spilled out of the shrine into eight big army tents.

By 1948 the congregation had so outgrown its tents and Quonset huts that it began to pray for a permanent sanctuary.

Spurred on by a twenty thousand dollar restoration and re-construction gift from the Presbyterian Commission on Ecumenical Mission and Relations, these incredible Christian refugees, so recently penniless and homeless, raised a hundred thousand dollars of their own, and began to build a stone cathedral. Women and children cleared the ground, swarming over it like basket-carrying ants. The men carried the stone from the quarry themselves, and the church rose and was finished.

But that was in 1950. Three weeks after the dedication service the Communists struck from the north, and the refugees were refugees once more. For days Christians in Seoul hid Dr. Han from the Communists. Five hundred pastors and Christian leaders were killed, but Dr. Han escaped and made his way south, where he was joined by many members of his congregation.

In Pusan, once again, Dr. Han and his refugee church members prayed and worked for a sanctuary in which they might worship God, and, once again, they built it out of stone. It became the largest Christian congregation in Pusan, and they called it, remembering their church in Seoul, the Church of Eternal Joy.

When devastated Seoul was liberated once more, the Pusan congregation joyfully prepared for the three hundred mile journey back from their refugee homes in Pusan to the temporary homes they had established in Seoul. But what would become of the church they had built in Pusan?

"It is not right," they said, "to leave this house of God empty." So families in the congregation covenanted together that they would not return to Seoul until each had found and won for Christ replacements for themselves in the Pusan church!

To thousands of refugees who have made their ragged way to freedom, Pastor Han's Church of Eternal Joy is more than a church. It is a haven of refuge, a feeding station, a job placement agency. It is an orphanage and a school.

Today the church supports forty-one full time evangelists and has established more than thirty new churches. And its outreach knows no national boundaries. In 1956 it sent a young Korean couple to Thailand as Presbyterian missionaries to work with the Church of Christ in Thailand.

What a record for a church of refugees who so recently had lost everything they owned in the world!

To the casual observer, like the American at the armistice line, such zeal and determination are inexplicable. "I cannot understand these Koreans" he says. Far more inexplicable to the Christian observer is how these same zealous and determined Korean Christians have allowed themselves to become so tragically divided in the years since the war. Where else in the world, for example, is there a Jesus Presbyterian Church and a Christ Presbyterian Church, and neither in fellowship with the other? Is Jesus Christ divided?

The divisions in the Korean church cut deep. There is, of course, the sharp line that separates Rome from the rest of Christendom. The Roman Catholic church in Korea is small, compared with the Protestant, but it is growing rapidly. It nearly trebled its membership between 1953 and 1960, according to reported statistics. At the present time there are almost three times as many Protestants as Catholics: about 1,300,000 Protestants, and 450,000 Catholics.

The familiar separation of Protestants into denominational families is an additional division within the Korean church. The following table shows the major denominations with the number of their adherents. Full church membership is considerably smaller.

1962

Presbyterians	775,000
Methodists	235,000
Holiness	96,000
Seventh-day Adventist	64,000
Salvation Army	25,000
Baptist	12,000
Assemblies of God	8,000
Episcopal (Anglican)	5,600
Churches of Christ	4,500
Nazarene	3,000
Korean Evangelical Mission	350
Lutheran	60

1,228,510

Denominational separations are not in themselves crippling divisions. The families of Protestantism have learned how to work together, and in Korea relationships have been most amiable. Presbyterians and Methodists, for example, very early reached a working agreement to avoid cutthroat competition. They divided rural Korea geographically between them, so that for many years a Presbyterian moving into Methodist territory almost automatically became a Methodist, and vice versa. Since 1919 the major denominations have been organized for co-operation through the Korean National Christian Council, which in recent years has represented about 75 per cent of the peninsula's Protestants.

But ever since the war in 1950, the Korean church has been struck with a plague of virulent schisms that have hurt her far more than any Communist invasion. Presbyterians have split into four rival factions. The Methodists have divided twice, but are successfully reunited again. Both the Baptists and the Holiness Church have been pulled apart by factional disputes.

Some excuse these schisms as only natural in Korea where division is a national tradition. Buddhists have split into open warfare between married priests and unmarried priests. The sedate Confucianists are split in two, fighting over robes in the temple. Factionalism in Korea's political parties has weakened the nation for centuries. Even the Seoul Symphony Orchestra split recently in a dispute over directors.

But however natural it may be for Korea, schism is not natural in the church of Jesus Christ. At Taegu, as the General Assembly of the Presbyterian Church in Korea began to divide, tempers rose, voices were lifted, and at one point elders and ministers came to blows in the aisles. A policeman was brought in from the street to restore order, and as he came forward he wept.

"Brothers," he cried, "I am only a policeman, but I am also a Christian, and I know that such things ought not to be. You are bringing shame to the name of Jesus Christ."

Disunity in the church, however, should not be allowed to blind the eyes of the observer to Korean Christianity's continuing, almost incredible vitality. They are divided, these Korean Christians, but still unconquerable. All during the decade of division, and in spite of its tragic schisms, the church continued to grow. In 1945, at the end of World

War II, the Protestant community numbered less than half a million persons; by 1961 it was approaching a million and a half. It doubled in number between 1950 and 1960.

Korean theological schools are crowded with more theological students than any other country in Asia, Africa, or Latin America. Churches are crowded. Attendance at a Korean church is always considerably larger than the membership of the church.

Some say the secret of this outflowing vitality is the evangelistic zeal of the Korean Christians. There have been congregations in Korea where new believers were not admitted to membership until they had proved their faith by winning at least one other person to Christ. Evangelism is not left to the professionals in Korea. Every Christian is expected to be an evangelist. But what, in turn, is the secret of this evangelistic, witnessing enthusiasm?

Some say it is the fervency in prayer. Before dawn, at four-thirty in the morning in summer, five-thirty in winter, groups of Christians will make their way to church to pray.

"How many come out to prayer meeting in your church?" a visitor asked a Korean pastor.

"About a hundred," he said.

"Oh," said the visitor, unimpressed, "we get that many out on Wednesday evenings in our own church back home in Oakland."

The pastor looked puzzled. "Wednesday evening?" he said. "I thought you meant prayer meeting. We have eight hundred at our Wednesday evening service!"

Prayer meeting to the Korean Christian is the pre-dawn circle of prayer, and it is indubitably a part of the secret of the church's strength, for it is a witness, in its way, to the presence of the Holy Spirit in the lives of the believers. There is a pentecostal ferment in all of Korea's churches, whether Methodist or Presbyterian or Baptist, that instead of weakening them has enriched their traditional disciplines with a glowing spiritual fervor.

Some say that the secret of the vitality of the Korean church is its devotion to the Word of God. Even years ago, Dr. A. J. Brown observed, "If there are any other Christians in the world who are more familiar with the Scriptures than the Korean Christians, I have not had the pleasure of meeting them."

Others say that the secret is the church's spirit of self-support and self-reliance, a tradition that was instilled in it from its early missionary beginnings. "We do not want to be rice Christians," Korean converts said. Stewardship had become an ingrained part of their Christian faith.

A story is told of a family of refugees making their painful way back to their home village after the Communist invasions. The home was gone; the church destroyed. But five bags of rice were still left under the courtyard where the family had buried them before fleeing south. It was all they had left, but the little Methodist family carefully set aside three of the precious bags of rice as a thank offering for their deliverance, giving them for the rebuilding of the church.

While some suggest evangelistic zeal or fervency in prayer, others stress devotion to the Word of God, or earnest stewardship as answers to the persistent question: Why is the church in Korea, in spite of all its weaknesses, still so strong? The strength of the church really can only be understood, however, in terms of the steadfast faith of individual Christians—Christians such as Major Noh.

Yong-Soo Noh was a major in the Korean Salvation Army. When the Communists swept through Kaesong in 1950 they took him prisoner and beat him and finally brought him out to give him one last chance for life. "Give up your faith in Christ," they said, "and we will set you free."

Major Noh drew himself up—like the officer he was in an army the Communists will never understand. With a Bible in one hand and hymnbook in the other, he answered "You can shoot me, I know, but alive or dead, I am still Jesus Christ's man."

Korea's Christian can differ, and they can die, but alive or dead they are Jesus Christ's men and Jesus Christ's women. And insofar as they are his, they are unconquerable.

3 | CHRISTIAN BEGINNINGS

As long as there have been Korean christians, there have been Koreans ready to die for their faith. When the Japanese Napoleon, Hideyoshi, invaded Korea in 1592—ravaging it so completely that "not even earthworms could live"—he was accompanied by a general, Yukinaga Konishi, who was a Roman Catholic convert. As a present for his daughter-in-law, Konishi sent two Korean prisoners back to Japan to serve in her household. One of them was "the son of the Secretary to the King of Corai," according to Father Luis Frois, a sixteenth century Portuguese missionary to Japan. "But the good lady," Father Frois wrote, "was moved by pity at seeing such young and noble boys reduced to a servile condition . . . she gave them to the Church, sending the Secretary's son to the Seminary. . . ."

Exiles and prisoners, and many of them soon to be martyrs—these were the first Korean Christian. In 1596 Father Frois reported three hundred converts from among the prisoners from "Corai" who were being held in Nagasaki. By 1608 Koreans had been ordained to the priesthood in Japan, and the Jesuits were planning to use them to carry the gospel back to their Korean homeland. But all plans to enter Korea from Japan died on the crosses of the martyrs in the bloody persecutions that began in 1614 (and continued intermittently until the dawn of the twentieth century).

The only Christian priest to enter Korea in that early period, and probably the first ever to set foot on its shores, was a Jesuit chaplain, Gregório de Céspedes. He was sent over from Japan at the request of General Konishi to care for the Catholic soldiers in his army. Father de Céspedes landed in Korea in 1594, but he was a chaplain to the Japanese, not a missionary to Korea, and as far as is known he never spoke to any Koreans in his short two months in the land.

Almost two hundred years passed before the Christian faith at last reached Koreans in their homeland, and then it came from China, not from Japan. As early as 1631 a member of the annual Korean embassy to Peking carried back with him to Seoul a copy of a book by a Jesuit missionary stationed in Peking, Matthew Ricci's True Doctrine of the Lord of Heaven. But for almost a century and a half, Roman Catholic books brought into the country were ignored. Beginning about 1777, however, a group of Korean scholars rediscovered the books, studied them, and even began to try to practice their teachings. In 1783 they commissioned a traveler to Peking to ask the Jesuits there for clearer information about the startling new faith. The man so commissioned, Sung-Heun Lee, did all they asked and more. He not only met a priest; he was converted and baptized. He returned in the spring of 1784, bringing books and crosses and the faith back with him. Baptized as Peter (Pierre) Lee, he was the first Korean Christian in his homeland.

The Catholic Century

The next hundred years, from 1784 to 1884, have been called "The century of Roman Catholic missions." It was a hundred years of heroism and faith, of persecutions and martyrdoms. It began with the first convert, but ominously, it also began with the first government edict against Christianity. Korea was still the Hermit Kingdom and wanted no penetration of foreign thought.

More than four hundred Korean Christian were publicly martyred for their faith in the first ten years of this Catholic century, and still no missionary had been able to penetrate the forbidden land. The first to do so was James Chu, a Chinese priest who entered in 1794. He hid from the authorities for months but finally gave himself up to protect his fellow believers. He was put to death in 1801.

The first Western missionary to penetrate the Hermit Kingdom was Father Pierre Maubant, who crawled through the sewers into the border city of Euiju in December, 1835. Four years later he was dead, beheaded on the sands of the Han River, along with two other European priests who had joined him. In the last great persecution of 1866, more than two thousand Korean Catholics gave their lives for Christ.

At the end of the first one hundred years of Roman Catholic missions in Korea, though there were said to be some 17,500 believers still alive, they had been so scattered and frightened and driven underground that Protestant missionaries coming into the country at that time found almost no

33

trace of them. The Roman Catholic Church in Korea, as such, had virtually ceased to exist.

But the Catholic faith survived. Not even its severest opponents could stamp it out. The most feared persecutor of the church in that century of martyrdom was the regent, the antiforeign, anti-Christian Tai Won Kun. It was at the orders of this man of blood that the church had been almost annihilated in 1866. But when he died some thirty years later, the faith, so far from being dead, had moved into his own home. His wife had become a Christian, baptized secretly at night by Bishop Mutel, who twice crept into the persecutor's palace, once to baptize her and once to give her Holy Communion. The year they buried the Tai Won Kun, 1898, there were forty thousand Roman Catholics in Korea.

Early Protestant Effort

The earliest, intermittent Protestant attempts to enter Korea were based on the belief that the most effective witness in that hermetically sealed land would be the witness of the Word of God, the Bible. The first Protestant visitors, therefore, gave themselves to Scripture distribution, an aspect of missionary witness that Roman Catholic missionaries did not stress.

In 1832, three years before the first European Catholic missionary crossed the Korean border, a Protestant missionary, a German named Carl Gutzlaff, sailed along the west coast for forty days or more, trying to witness to the Koreans he met and distributing religious tracts and Chinese Bibles that his friend Robert Morrison, the first Protestant missionary to China, had given him. He managed with some difficulty to get the Lord's Prayer translated into Korean, but it was not received with any great joy. The captain of Gutzlaff's ship reported that the Koreans repeatedly drew their fore-fingers across their throats to emphasize the great danger that the presence of foreigners meant to them all.

The year of terror for Korea's Catholics was also the year of Korea's first Protestant martyr. The Rev. Robert J. Thomas had spent two-and one-half months in 1865 on Korea's west coast, studying Korean and distributing Bibles. He returned safely by Chinese junk to China. But when he went back to Korea the next year, his ship—the American vessel "General Sherman"—was burned by fear-stricken Koreans in the river near Pyongyang, and Thomas was killed in the very act of offering a Bible to the man who beheaded him.

In the years that followed other attempts were made by Protestant missionaries to bring the Word of God to Korea, but none was more successful than the effort made by a pair of Scottish missionaries in Manchuria, John Ross and John McIntyre, who have been called the "Wycliffes of Korea." These two men, though neither one set foot in Korea until years later, baptized the first Korean Protestant converts in Manchuria in 1876, and made the first Korean translation of the New Testament during the years, 1882-1887.

Among the four Koreans baptized in 1876 was a man named Sang-Yoon Suh, who with his fellow converts began a work of partnership in pioneering with the missionaries that has been a mark of the Korean church ever since. Korean Christians, it has been observed, have always been one jump ahead of the missionaries. Like their Roman Catholic brethren before them, Suh and his colleagues made their way back into Korea and began winning their own converts before any missionary was able to take up permanent work in their forbidden land.

The first resident Protestant missionary to Korea was the physician, Horace N. Allen. A red-headed six-footer, he had transferred from the Presbyterian mission in China and landed, seasick and weary, at Inchon on September 20, 1884. Undiscouraged by his first impressions of the country ("a motley place of slab shanties, mud huts, shacks, and fresh earth"), he pressed on to Seoul where he was received gladly by the United States Minister and was promptly appointed physician to the American legation. His appointment secured his safety, since there was still no "toleration of religion" clause in Korea's foreign treaties, and the ancient edict against missionaries was still binding. Christianity was an outlawed religion.

But unknown to Allen, there were already Protestants in Seoul. About that time, Sang-Yoon Suh, one of the converts from Manchuria, reached the capital. He had come across the Yalu in 1883, but had stopped at his home on the west coast before proceeding to Seoul to distribute Christian literature. There he discovered that American missionaries had just arrived, but he did not reveal himself to them. Instead, with characteristic Korean loyalty to an old teacher, Suh wrote John Ross, asking the Scot to come down and baptize the more than a hundred believers who had been won by the Korean evangelists. Mr. Ross, however, was unable to go, since open missionary work by foreigners was still out of the question.

But less than three months later, the gates of the Hen Kingdom were dramatically opened to the gospel. A plot against the conservatives in the Korean court exploded into violence on the night of Dec. 4, 1884. Scores of the King's councilors were murdered. The Queen's nephew, Prince Yong-Ik Min, lay dying in a pool of blood, seven sword cuts on his head and body. Over the objections of fourteen palace physicians, who were about to pour black pitch into the patient's wounds, the foreign doctor, Horace Allen, was summoned, and raced across town with an escort of fifty soldiers. For three months he fought to save the prince's life. Failure meant the end of his work in Korea, but the prince recovered. A grateful king promptly appointed Allen as physician to the royal court and allowed him to open a hospital in Seoul, sponsored by the government "in co-operation with a benevolent society in America." Indirect and cautious though the phrasing of the decree was, it was the first official approval by the Korean government of missionary work in Korea.

Five days before the new hospital opened its doors, the first ordained Protestant missionaries landed at Inchon. It was on Easter morning, April 5, 1885, that the Rev. Horace Grant Underwood, a Presbyterian, and the Rev. and Mrs. Henry G. Appenzeller, Methodists, arrived together in Korea. Mr. Appenzeller wrote, "We came here on Easter. May He who on that day burst asunder the bars of death, break the bonds that bind the people, and bring them to the light and liberty of God's children."

Appenzeller's prayer was soon answered, and much of the initiative in breaking the bonds of which he wrote so movingly came from the Koreans themselves.

The first convert in Seoul, for example, stole a Bible to get converted, as Dr. Allen often jestingly said. To put it more accurately, he borrowed it against the strong advice of the missionary. It was at the height of the 1884 palace revolt that Tohsa Noh, Allen's second language teacher, borrowed portions of his Chinese New Testament. "You'll have your head cut off if they find you reading that book," Allen told him. But the man persisted, and later he came to talk to Mr. Underwood concerning his reading and to borrow more Christian literature. When he finally asked Mr. Underwood to baptize him, the missionary told him bluntly, "You are going contrary to the law of your country. If you take this step there will be no turning back." But again Noh persisted, and on July 11, 1886, the persistent Mr. Noh became the first Korean Protestant ever baptized in his own country.

Meanwhile, just one year after his prayer in the harbor at Inchon, Henry Appenzeller had given an Easter baptism to the first Methodist convert in Korea, a Japanese. In the summer of 1887 he baptized two Korean students at Pai Chai academy, which he had recently started, and a few months later he baptized the first Korean woman ever to become a Protestant. By the fall of 1888 the Methodist mission was prepared to license two Koreans as the first local preachers in the Hermit Kingdom.

To the Korean Christians belongs the credit for establishing and organizing the first Protestant church. Presbyterian and Methodist missionaries had been holding church services together in Seoul since June, 1885, but no church was organized for fear of offending the government. What a surprise then it must have been when, toward the close of 1886, a

Korean from a remote coastal village made his way to the Underwood home and asked the missionary to come and baptize believers there. No missionary had ever visited the village, but for months a little group had been meeting together for worship. In all Korea the missionaries had only one baptized convert. Whence, then, came this already gathered congregation of Christians? What was behind this "mysteriously sudden growth" of the Korean church?

The unexpected visitor was Sang-Yoon Suh. He had been reluctant to come to the American missionaries, but now, unwilling to wait any longer for John Ross to come from Manchuria, he wanted his converts in Sorai baptized. Could the missionary come at once? Mr. Underwood, no more than Ross, could travel into the forbidden interior on such short notice. But Sang-Yoon Suh did not despair. The next spring he appeared again, this time bringing the converts with him! They were received with great pleasure. The whole mission was convened to examine them, and three men were found ready for baptism. Before the service the men were solemnly warned of the risks involved. "We are ready," they replied, "to stand by our faith to the death." So with a Methodist, Homer Hulbert, guarding the door for fear of discovery, Mr. Underwood gave Presbyterian baptism to the Sorai believers. In the fall he visited Sorai and baptized seven more.

This obscure little hamlet has been rightly called "the cradle of Protestant Christianity in Korea," by Dr. George L. Paik. Its tiny church, first in the peninsula, gave a distinctive stamp to the amazing growth of the Protestant church that followed. Started by the Korean Christians themselves, it was self-supporting from the beginning. Moreover, it called the missions to a policy of rural itineration that became foundational in the rise of the Korean church.

The organization of the first city churches was more formal. By providential circumstance John Ross arrived in Seoul just in time to accompany Mr. Underwood through the unlighted alleys of the capital to a small room where they helped organize the city's first Presbyterian church, now the Saimoonan Church. A few weeks later, on October 9, 1887, Mr. Appenzeller held the first Methodist "public service for Koreans" in the Bethel Chapel, which has now become the great Chung Dong Methodist Church.

It was no easy thing to become a Christian in those days. For the men, the great obstacle was Korea's Confucian tradition of ancestor worship. For a son to become a Christian was to betray his father and to rob the dead of the filial reverences that were their due. No greater sin could be imagined in a land whose whole social fabric was shaped by Confucian patterns. Male converts were insulted and stoned, and often disinherited by their families, for joining the outlawed foreign sect. And over all, of course, hung the shadows of the great Christian massacres in the not too distant past. Even as late as 1901, five or six hundred Catholics were killed on Cheju Island.

Women, too, were beaten and sometimes killed for believing. To believe was to admit another loyalty than to the husband, and this was contrary to Confucian teaching. Korea's social customs, as well, made faith difficult for the women. At this time it was not proper for a woman's face to be seen by any man except her husband. In the church women were hidden from the men by a partitioning curtain. But how, then, could a woman be baptized? This is the way the Methodist missionary, Dr. W. B. Scranton, solved the problem for the first woman baptized as a Protestant in North Korea, Mrs. Samtok Chun, wife of the royal councilor. She describes the strangeness of her baptism as follows:

"Dr. Scranton asked me if I did not wish to be baptized. I replied that I should like to . . . but that since the customs of our country did not allow a man to see a woman face to face, I didn't see how such a ceremony could be performed. . . . He replied, 'That being the case, let us do it this way. Put up a curtain in the middle of a room, make a hole in the curtain large enough for you to put your head partly through and we will have the Baptism service right there.' I arranged the room as he requested and then received baptism, with all due reverence, through the aperture."

The first five years of Protestant effort in Korea, up to 1890, were almost entirely restricted to the port cities of Seoul, Inchon, and Pusan, which, with two other ports, had been opened by treaty for foreign residence. Isolated groups of Christians in the interior, as at Sorai and Euiju, were visited at considerable risk and only at long intervals by the early missionaries. In the 1890s, however, the Protestant church moved inland, and new mission groups arrived to share in the expansion.

The first center of this inland expansion was Pyongyang, the ancient northern capital founded in the days of David and Solomon, whose reputation for wickedness earned it the name of "the Sodom of Korea." After a number of earlier exploratory trips, the Rev. S. A. Moffett moved into Pyongyang in 1893, becoming the first resident Protestant missionary in the forbidden interior. He was stoned in the streets but stayed at his post, and early the next year he baptized seven men, the foundation of a work that was for a time to become the largest Presbyterian mission station in the world.

At the same time the Methodists realized that their characteristic circuit system of organization was ideally suited for the penetration of the interior, and they opened up inland circuits in Pyongyang and Chunju. In 1894 Methodist believers built the first Korean Protestant chapel in the land at Inchon. Characteristically, the Koreans had raised the entire cost themselves—thirty dollars! The chapel was a twelve by twenty foot building with straw thatched roof, mud walls, and mud floors.

It was also in this decade that other missionary agencies joined the Presbyterians and Methodists in Korea. As early as 1885 Anglicans of the Church Missionary Society in China sent two independent Chinese evangelists to work in Pusan. For five years they labored there but had no converts. They withdrew when the Church of England formally established a mission to Korea with the consecration of the Rev. C. J. Corfe as "first Missionary Bishop of Corea." Bishop Corfe reached Korea in 1890 accompanied by a young Episcopal doctor, E. B. Landis. The Anglicans voluntarily took upon themselves the "seal of Apostolic poverty." They received no salaries and held all things in common, "living a common life on a small common fund." They refrained from any direct evangelism for six years, preparing themselves by a quiet study of the language and habits of the people. On Christmas Eve, 1896, the days of preparation at last over, they baptized their first Koreans, enrolled their first catechumens, and the next day held the first Korean service from the Book of Common Prayer.

In October, 1889, the Presbyterian Church of Victoria, Australia, opened a mission to Korea. Within six months its pioneer missionary, the gifted J. Henry Davies, was dead of smallpox and pneumonia, but his dying so aroused the churches of Australia that the result was new commitment to the cause of Christ in Korea.

Southern Presbyterians (Presbyterian Church in the United States) entered Korea in force in 1892 with seven missionaries. The first to reach Korea was Miss Linnie Davis who reached Seoul on October 18, 1892. Arriving late, she found the city gates already closed. There was nothing else to do but pull her up by ropes over the top of the forty-foot stone wall. Southern Presbyterians took as their field of operation the unreached provinces of the far southwest.

Independent Baptist work in Korea was begun in late 1889 by a Canadian, Malcolm C. Fenwick. He was a tireless evangelist, patterning his work after the example of the China Inland Mission but emphasizing the witness of Korean Christians rather than foreign missionaries. He was joined for a time (1894-1900) by American Baptist missionaries from Dr. A. J. Gordon's Clarendon Street Baptist Church in Boston. The work of these early Baptists has now been inherited by the Southern Baptist mission in Korea.

Southern Methodists were brought into Korea by the entreaties of a young Korean aristocrat, Chi-Ho Yoon, scion of a noble family, who had been converted while a student in Shanghai in 1887. Later he studied in America at Vanderbilt University (Tennessee) and Emory University (Georgia).

After graduation, longing for the conversion of his country and eager to stir up the American church to more intensive work there, he gave several hundred dollars to his college president to be used, he said, "when the Southern Methodists are ready to open a mission in Korea." They responded in 1896. Baron Chi-Ho Yoon, it should be noted, was the uncle of a venerated president of the Republic of Korea, Dr. Po-Sun Yoon.

"Canada and Korea were linked together by William J. Mackenzie," commented later missionaries when describing the work of the first Canadian Presbyterian pioneer. It was in 1893 that Mackenzie threw in his lot with the Christians at Sorai, living with them in their tiny village. At his suggestion they began to build the first Presbyterian church in Korea, for the congregation had grown too large for the little Christian homes in which they had been meeting. One week after the chapel was completed, June, 1895, Mackenzie was dead of a fever, but not before he had enthusiastically celebrated the anniversary of his arrival in Korea by raising a flag "emblazoned with St. George's Cross" over the place of worship. This was the beginning of the tradition that Protestant churches in Korea should be marked by the sign of the cross. In 1898 the Canadian Presbyterian Church opened a mission to Korea—Mackenzie had come to the field independently—and pioneers like Dr. Robert G. Grierson began work in the northeast. In 1925 church union brought about 70 per cent of Canada's Presbyterians into the United Church of Canada and with them came the Korean mission. Canadian missionaries are now stationed in Seoul, Iri, Pusan, and Wonju.

The Seventh-day Adventists began work in Korea in 1903. In 1907 the Oriental Missionary Society entered the peninsula for evangelistic efforts that have resulted in the growth of Korea's third largest Protestant denomination, the Holiness Church. The Salvation Army opened its Korean operations in 1908.

Co-operation

These were the first Protestant groups to enter Korea and they are, in the main, the major denominations now at work. There are, however, a number of less well known groups in Korea, most of which entered the country at the end of World War II. All told, there are some forty-two Protestant missions and societies. It is this profusion of Protestant agencies, added to the present sad splintering of denominations, that obscures the emphatically ecumenical nature of Protestant beginnings in the country.

The four different Presbyterian bodies, for example, (now United Presbyterian, Presbyterian U.S., Australian Presbyterian, and United Church of Canada) agreed at once to forget their divisions at home and join in forming only one Presbyterian church in Korea. For this purpose, as early as 1889, Presbyterian missionaries established an organ of intermission co-operation that came to be called the Presbyterian Council. Likewise the two Methodist missions (Northern and Southern) early agreed to unite in educational and literary work.

By 1892 enthusiasm for co-operation overleaped confessional boundaries and brought Methodists and Presbyterians into an agreement to divide the Korean peninsula into non-com-

45

petitive geographical spheres of influence. As finally hammered out some fifteen years later, this remarkable comity agreement saw about four thousand Methodists become Presbyterians overnight as rural areas were denominationally redistricted, and about the same number of Presbyterians similarly awoke to discover that they had suddenly become Methodists.

In schools and hospitals, as well, Protestant co-operation vaulted over denominational barriers. Describing an experiment in union educational work in Pyongyang in 1905, Dr. W. M. Baird wrote, "The need was so great that we [i.e. Presbyterians and Methodists] did not wait for a well developed scheme or constitution for the control of the school before commencing. We simply commenced to co-operate by co-operating. . . . It is better to work shoulder to shoulder than in disunion and weakness and moral defeat." The result of this pioneer ecumenical spirit was the foundation of Union Christian College (Soongsil University), whose first two graduates, three years later, were the first in Korea to receive college diplomas.

Soon, an even wider union brought Anglican, Methodist, and Presbyterian physicians into Severance Union Medical College and Hospital in Seoul. And though it was not founded until the middle of the next decade, Korea's most ambitious union project, Chosen Christian University (now Yonsei) should be mentioned. Ultimately it brought Koreans, Americans, Canadians, Britishers, and Australians into co-operation, with Methodists, Presbyterians, Anglicans, the United Church of Canada, and even the United Church of Christ in the Philippines sharing in the project in one way or another. Its founder and first president, fittingly enough, was the pioneer who thirty years earlier had first penetrated the Hermit Kingdom, Horace G. Underwood.

In literary and translation work, too, the missionaries pooled their talents and resources irrespective of denominational ties. As early as 1889 they had organized the Korean Religious Tract Society (now the Christian Literature Society) to publish a wide range of interdenominational literature. The twentieth century began with their greatest literary achievement, the completion of the Korean translation of the New Testament only sixteen years after the arrival of the first missionary. A few years later a Union Hymn Book was published, so in scripture and in song the denominations were united.

The high point of the tide to union was the year 1905-06. A summer Bible Conference for all missionaries had been held for the first time, taking their minds off their surface differences and focusing them on the deep truths of the Book that brings Christians close to Christ and to each other, the Word of God. A committee meeting of Methodists and Presbyterians was called to discuss union efforts in evangelism and theological education. Swept along by the spirit of harmony and good will that prevailed among the members, the group unanimously accepted a motion by the Southern Presbyterian pioneer, Dr. W. D. Reynolds, declaring that ". . . the time is ripe for the establishment of one Korean National Church, to be called the Church of Christ in Korea."

The enthusiasm thus generated brought the six major missions then at work in Korea (Northern and Southern Presbyterian, Northern and Southern Methodist, Australian and

47

Canadian Presbyterian) into a General Council of Evangelical Missions in Korea that took as its aim "co-operation in Christian work and eventually the organization of one Evangelical Church in Korea." A mass meeting of delegates, representing 196 missionaries or about 95 per cent of the total Protestant force in Korea at that time, unanimously ratified the Council's ambitious aim at the second annual meeting the next year. It was the high watermark of union effort in Korea.

From that time on, however, interest in organic union of the churches waned and was replaced by intensive denominational expansion, tempered by friendly co-operation. Church union, it was argued, cannot be dictated by missions from abroad but must be the free choice of the national and independent Korean churches that they were about to establish. Disappointment over the fading of a magnificent dream gave way to heady excitement over the unprecedentedly rapid rise of great Korean churches.

4 | A NATION ON THE RUN TO GOD

DR. JOHN R. MOTT RETURNED FROM A TRIP TO THE
Far East in 1907 declaring that "If the present work on the
part of the co-operating missions in Korea is adequately sus-
tained and enlarged in the immediate future, Korea will be
the first nation in the non-Christian world to become a
Christian nation."

Such soaring optimism contrasts sharply with a harsh judgment circulating among Korean university students in 1960:
"Buddhism died with the fall of the Koryu dynasty in the
fourteenth century; Confucianism died with the fall of the
Yi dynasty in 1910; and now Christianity is dying with the
fall of Syngman Rhee."

Both Mott and the Korean students were wrong. Korea
still is not a Christian nation; and Christianity in Korea did
not die with the resignation of a Christian president.

But Dr. Mott's optimism was solidly based on a record in-
flow of believers that carried the Protestant church in Korea
from a handful of scattered believers in 1885 to a total com-

munity of some fifty thousand adherents by 1905, and to more than two hundred thousand by 1909, the twenty-fifth anniversary of the opening of Protestant work in Korea. It was a record unmatched in the Christian world of that time, save perhaps in Uganda. By 1935-36, after fifty years of Protestant work, total church membership had grown to 374,583, to which could be added some 300,000 others, making a Christian community of 674,000. Today the total is still soaring and stands at about 1,300,000 Protestant adherents. Between 1905 and 1960 the Protestant church grew ten times as fast as the population. The number of Koreans increased by about 250 per cent, but the number of Protestants increased by 2,600 per cent, doubling in the five years between 1905 and 1910, increasing sixfold in the next thirty years, and doubling again in the twenty-five years between 1935 and 1960.

The pattern of this growth in the church has been complex. Geographically it followed Korea's traditional culture flow from the northwest to the central and southern regions, with the latest, and sometimes the highest flowering in the conservative valleys of the southeast. This was true of the spread of Buddhism, first, and later of Confucianism. It now seems to be true of Christianity. After twenty years of Protestant work, for example, the northwest, though containing only one-fourth of the Protestant missionaries in Korea, reported about half of the baptisms, adherents, and church contributions of the whole country. Today organized Christianity is nonexistent in North Korea, and how permanently the Communist occupation will cripple the church there only the future will tell. Meanwhile, as in the ancient culture pat-

tern, the areas of most rapid indigenous (as opposed to refugee) growth seem to be in the southeast.

Chronologically, Korean church growth divides into eight
periods of advance and recession. For the first twenty years
of missionary work there was a steady rise in membership
(1884-1904). Then came a meteoric rise, "the great ingathering," and for a while Korea seemed, as someone said, "a
nation on the run to God" [1] (1905-1910). But suddenly the
pace slackened and the church entered a decade of decline
(1911-1919). Two short periods characterized the twenties:
a revival of growth [2] (1920-24) and another recession (1925-
28). Then, once again, the church entered a period of spectacular progress [3] (1929-1937) that carried it up to the Far
Eastern beginnings of World War II. From that time on,
Korean statistics become even more chaotic, but the general
outline of continuing waves of advance and recession remain
fairly clear: a wartime recession (1937-1945) and another advance [4] (1945-1960). To update Dr. A. W. Wasson's thirty-
year-old description of church growth in Korea, the tide has
been at the flood four times and thrice it has ebbed since the
turn of the century.

Some observers find in the troubled state of the nation an
explanation for the phenomenal growth of the Korean
church. A five-hundred-year-old dynasty was crumbling to its
close. Korea's freedom hung on the balance of power between its three mighty neighbors—Japan, China, and Russia.
When Japan defeated China in 1895 and Russia ten years
later, the pear blossom throne was doomed. A weeping king
accepted Japan's protectorate in 1905 and was forced from
his throne in 1910. Korea had become a Japanese colony.

As centuries before when an empire fell and men lifted up their eyes to look for a City of God, so now in Korea, men troubled by their times looked for more eternal things. Some came to the church for refuge. Some came because the church was Western. "Japan's power lies not in herself," they said, in effect, "but in her rapid westernization. Why take this power secondhand from Japan when perhaps we can get it firsthand from the Westerners already among us, the missionaries?" Others came because the old religions had obviously failed the nation, and the new religion might mean hope. Besides, Christianity did not deny much that people had loved in the old beliefs. Like Confucianism, it taught righteousness and revered learning; like Buddhism, it sought purity and promised a future life; like the shamanists, Christians believed in answered prayer and miracles.

The Great Revival

All these explanations are true, but they can never quite account for the white-hot, almost volcanic upheavals that shook the church in the first decade of the twentieth century.

It was a spiritual revival, explosive and spectacular, sweeping through the peninsula from 1903 to 1907, that touched off the massive ingathering of the church and permanently stamped its character with revivalistic fervor. A British lord, writing later in the London Times, compared the "extraordinary manifestations of power in Korea" with the revivals of John Wesley.

The revival began quietly enough in a week of prayer and Bible study for missionaries in Wonsan, led by a Methodist physician from Canada, R. A. Hardie. In the course of his

Bible studies, Dr. Hardie felt compelled by the Spirit to go before his fellow missionaries and later before a Korean congregation to confess "with shame and confusion," as he reported to his mission, "my own pride, hardness of heart and lack of faith. . . ."

From Wonsan revivalism spread and reached its climax at a great evening meeting in Pyongyang, in 1907. Of this meeting, Dr. W. N. Blair, one of the leaders, wrote:

"Then began a meeting the like of which I had never seen before, nor wish to see again unless in God's sight it is absolutely necessary. Every sin a human being can commit was publicly confessed that night . . . guilty souls standing in the white light of that judgment, saw themselves as God saw them. We may have our theories of the advisability or undesirability of public confession of sin. I have had mine, but I know now that when the Spirit of God falls on guilty souls, there will be confession, and no power on earth can stop it."

Equally vivid was the description of a Korean minister, who said:

"It was a great sign and wonder. . . . I saw some struggling to get up, then falling back in agony. Others again bounded to their feet to rid their souls of some long-covered sin. It seemed unwise that such confessions be made. . . . But there was no help for it. We were under a mysterious and awful power, helpless—missionaries as well as Koreans."

The revival spread, the church grew. In five short years, beginning in Wonsan in 1903, the membership of the churches in Korea increased fourfold. No better argument had ever been made for the Christian faith than the cleansing transformation that the revival wrought in the lives of the believers.

Christians went from house to house confessing their sins to those whom they had wronged. Missionaries and Korean Christians, convicted together of their shortcomings, had never known a closer fellowship. The revival was the spiritual seal on the founding charter of the Korean church. As Koreans said afterwards to the missionaries, "Some of you go back to John Calvin, and some of you to John Wesley, but we can go back no further than 1907 when we first really knew the Lord Jesus Christ."

Korean Organization of the Church

Another factor in continuing and consolidating the growth of the church was its timely and effective organization for self-government. Multitudes were pouring into the church warmed by revival fires. Lest their emotions cool and they drift away, they had to be quickly challenged to growth and responsibility. Fortunately and wisely, leadership in the church passed from missionaries to Korean Christians just in time to face the converts with the challenge they needed. It was in time, too, to keep one door open for the free exercise of leadership, since Korea's loss of independence deprived her people of all other forms of self-government.

The first Koreans ordained to the Protestant ministry (as deacons) were two Methodists, Chang-Sik Kim and Pum-Keui Kim, who were thus authorized to baptize and perform marriages, but not to administer communion. Methodist organization of an independent Korean church followed considerably later, although a Korea Conference (Methodist,

North) was founded in 1908, and another (Methodist, South) in 1918. It was not until 1930 that the two united to form an autonomous Korean Methodist Church—"genuinely Christian, truly Methodist, and really Korean."

It is with the founding of the Presbyterian Church in Korea in 1907 that the age of independent self-government in the Korean church really begins. Up to that time all the highest church courts in the land had been organizations of the foreign missions—a Methodist Mission Conference, for example, or the Presbyterian Council, which was composed of all ordained Presbyterian missionaries in Korea and operated as an unofficial presbytery of somewhat dubious legal standing, ecclesiastically.

But at noon on September 17, 1907, the rap of the moderator's gavel announced the establishment of the first presbytery of the Korean Presbyterian Church, independent and self-governing. Membership was composed of forty Korean Christians and thirty-six foreign missionaries, representing Australian, Canadian, and American Presbyterian churches. By 1927 there were still thirty-six missionaries, but 172 Korean members.

The presbytery ordained seven men to the full ministry of the word and the sacraments, among them the brother of the Sorai pioneer, Sang-Yoon Suh. As the first ministers of the Korean church, all seven were urgently needed for Korea, but impelled by higher loyalties and firm in the conviction that a church is not a church without a mission, the infant church scrupulously set aside one of the seven as a foreign missionary—to the island of Cheju. His commissioning was dramatic. The man chosen for the mission, Poong-Ki Lee, was one who years earlier had joined the mob in savagely stoning a foreign missionary in the streets of Pyongyang. Now that same missionary, Dr. S. A. Moffett, just elected by the Korean presbytery as its first moderator, proudly commissioned the newly ordained minister. "Sixteen years ago he stoned me on the streets of Pyongyang," said Dr. Moffett, "and now he goes as the first missionary of the church in Korea."

When the Presbyterian Church in Korea organized its first General Assembly in 1912, it elected as moderator, Horace G. Underwood, whom it revered as founder of the church. Once again, as at the formation of the first presbytery, the Korean church felt that a forward step in church organization at home must be accompanied by a forward step in world outreach. The church had already sent missionaries to Cheju Island (1907), Japan (1908), and Siberia (1909), but in each case the mission had been to Koreans resident there. The first General Assembly, therefore, regarded its proceedings as incomplete until it had undertaken a genuinely "foreign" mission by commissioning three Koreans as its first missionaries to the Chinese in China. An important element in this Korean missionary program was the acceptance by the church of full financial responsibility for the missions. Their offering was not limited to the giving of life; it encompassed also the support of that life.

Self-government, thus, was no end in itself. Self-government was for witness, and this became a significant part of the forward surge of the church.

Christians gave not only of their tithes to evangelism, they tithed their time and they gave themselves. They found it the most natural thing in the world to speak to others about their new faith and about Jesus Christ. As one put it, "What else is there worthwhile talking about, anyway?" Sometimes the missionaries winced as new converts witnessed with more zeal than wisdom, but even then the witness was more often than not overruled for good. In one northern city, an observer reported, four old women were deeply impressed by a sermon about the palsied man who was carried to Jesus by four friends. They too had a friend, an old lady who not only refused to come to church herself but kept her daughters from becoming believers. The next Sunday they went to her house, picked her up and "carried her by main force to the church, which was crowded to the door. Nothing daunted, they passed her on over the heads of the people, right up to the front. Gradually, as she listened to the story of Jesus, her indignation melted into interest, and finally she became a believer."

It soon became obvious that the testimony of the Korean converts was far more effective as an evangelistic agency than the preaching of the missionaries. Mr. M. C. Fenwick, the independent Baptist missionary, trained a whole corps of Korean evangelists after the humiliating discovery that however hard he preached, "testifying in tears to the love of God in Christ . . . people simply laughed at me and said that was all well enough for me, a Westerner, but they were Coreans." One day he asked a Korean believer to testify and was astounded at the result. "I saw how his testimony gripped the people as mine had never done. . . . These Corean sinners listened that day to Mr. Kim because he, too, was a Corean. . . ."

So strong was the tide of Korean evangelism that an American reporter in Korea wrote that the missionaries no longer needed to give time to evangelism themselves, so busy were they "trying to keep up with the procession of native-made converts into the church. Every Christian becomes an evangelist."

Still a third factor in the rise of the church was its sturdy self-reliance in financial matters. The church was not only self-propagating and self-governing, it was self-supporting. In fact, one widely held theory of missionary strategy was based on the proposition that the church could not actually be self-governing until it was self-supporting. "It is as futile in Asia as it is everywhere else to imagine that real independence is compatible with financial dependence," wrote one mission board executive.

By 1908, out of 188 Presbyterian churches in Korea, 186 were entirely self-supporting, and it was not long before the Korean Christians were contributing more to the upbuilding of their church than they were receiving in missionary gifts from abroad. In the first twenty-five years of its work in Korea (1884-1909), the Presbyterian Board of Foreign Missions, as could be expected, spent five times as much in Korea as the infant Korean Presbyterian Church was able to contribute. In the next twenty-five years, however, Korean Christians matched the board dollar for dollar so that when, in 1934, the Korea Mission celebrated fifty years of service in Korea, board expenditures and Korean contributions over the years were almost equal.

Now, in nearly all the churches of Korea, the stewardship of Korean Christians far outstrips even the generous giving of their American friends. Methodist figures for 1960 show that of the 996 organized churches, 826 were fully self-supporting, and the other 170 were on only a half-subsidy. Korean Methodists themselves were contributing 95 per cent of the salaries of the pastors and Bible women. Such figures take on added impact when it is remembered that Korea's economy is predominantly rural, that the average farm is about four acres, and the average per capita annual income is about eighty dollars. Yet Korean Methodists give to their church an amount equal to seven dollars for every man, woman, and child in the church.

The Nevius Plan

Three of the factors cited above as contributing to the spectacular growth of the church in Korea—self-propagation, self-government, and self-support—are the three familiar pillars of a policy of missionary work that is often called the Nevius Plan, though as so summarized it did not originate with Nevius.

John L. Nevius was a missionary to China who paid a most significant visit to Korea at a time, 1890, when its missionaries were still feeling their way toward an over-all strategy for the evangelization of Korea. Nevius had become disillusioned with what he called the "old way" of carrying on missions—using foreign funds to hire national workers to build up the church. He proposed instead a "new way" that minimized as far as possible the use of paid national workers and advocated that the national church be independent and self-reliant from the beginning. He took the three familiar principles of self-propagation, self-government, and self-support and fashioned them into a uniquely disciplined pattern of missionary strategy which, as practiced rather widely in Korea, emphasized five major principles:

1. *Bible study.* The Bible was made the basis of all Christian work and was taught systematically in winter and summer Bible classes. It was religious education for all the people.

2. *Self-propagation.* Every Christian was expected to teach the faith to others, not as a professional evangelist but while carrying on his normal occupation.

3. *Self-government.* Groups of believers selected from among themselves their own unpaid "leaders"; these groups were organized into circuits served by paid "helpers," preferably but not necessarily supported by the groups themselves.

4. *Self-support.* Each group was expected to build its own church and call and support its own pastor. Until they were thus self-supporting, they met in Christian homes and shared the services of a circuit evangelist.

5. *Missionary itineration.* The missionary was to itinerate widely, with a Korean "helper," but avoided accepting pastorates of Korean churches.

See Brown p. 15. 51. 79;

The Nevius Plan has been widely praised and widely criticized. Criticism centers principally around the contention that the plan radically over-emphasizes self-support and makes money the mark of a church's maturity. On the other hand, Roland Allen, writing in *World Dominion*, compared the Nevius method unfavorably with "St. Paul's methods," chiding the Plan for not being radical enough. Self-government from the beginning, Allen insisted, is as important as self-support.

To such thoughtful objections, defenders of the Plan as practiced in Korea would probably reply: first, emphasis on self-support is only one of several equally important aspects of a total missionary strategy; second, while money is never the mark of the maturity of a church, it is often the cause of its downfall, and in the long run, to over-subsidize a younger church may prove to be a more tragic mistake than to under-supply it with foreign funds.

At any rate, whatever its merits and demerits may have been, the Nevius Plan was uniquely successful in Korea. There is no disputing the fact that the Korean church grew most rapidly in precisely those areas of the peninsula where the Nevius Plan was practiced most faithfully. Not a few have pointed out that the present period of schism in the church is also the period of easier access to foreign funds and discontinuance of the Nevius method.

New Relationships

The Nevius Plan, however, can no longer be considered the operative principle of mission or church policies in Korea. War first made it obsolete, and after the war new patterns of church relations arose to challenge its continuing validity.

For thiry-nine months, from 1950 to 1953, marching and counter-marching armies raked the peninsula from end to end. The church was razed and stripped and its people left hungry and homeless. The overwhelming relief and recon-struction needs of Korea after the war made at least a tempo-rary suspension of the principle of self-support inevitable. How could a congregation that had scraped and saved for years to build a church, only to see it burned before their eyes by the Communists, be denied help from abroad in building again?

At the same time a significant change in the world-wide

strategy of the Christian church was shifting emphasis away from self-support and encouraging the younger churches to "move beyond independence to interdependence." The 1948 conference of the International Missionary Council held at Whitby, Ontario, urged self-government and self-propagation, but was relatively silent about self-support. To some this appeared to be a backward step, a mere rationalization of the failure of most younger churches to attain self-support, and an excuse for further subsidization. To others it was a necessary corollary of the coming of age of the younger churches and a possible corrective of the danger of their drift into excessive nationalism.

Organizationally, too, the emphasis of the "new day in missions" was not on independence but on integration and interdependence. In Dr. Robert E. Speer's familiar figure of the mission as a scaffolding existing only for the erection of the building, the church, it was time for the scaffolding to come down. The church was built. Where once there had been only a mission and no church, then a mission and a growing church, now with the coming of age of the church, it was said that the third stage had been reached calling for a church and no mission. The mission, as such, was supposed to be absorbed or integrated into the life of the church.

For some this was no problem. The Anglican mission in Korea was the church in Korea, and always had been since the consecration of its first bishop. Likewise the church was the mission. Its bishops had all been missionary bishops: Charles John Corfe, the pioneer (1889-1904); Arthur Beresford Turner (1905-1910); Mark Napier Trollope (1910-1930), the "second founder" of the church and builder of the cathedral, who had been the first priest on Bishop Corfe's staff and had baptized the first convert; Cecil Cooper (1930-1955) who saw the number of Korean priests rise to eighteen in 1939, and then for them endured exile by the Japanese and capture by the Communists; and John C. S. Daly (1955-) who, before coming to Korea, had vigorously pioneered in building his African dioceses toward autonomy and independence within the Anglican communion. All these were missionary bishops, and church and mission were one.

Methodists, too, were integrated into one Korean body with the formation of the independent Korean Methodist Church in 1930. Previously missionaries and Koreans had worked together in the Northern and Southern Annual Conferences, which were responsible to the American churches. Now in the new organization missionaries accepted the jurisdiction of the Korean church and its general superintendent (later bishop).

Presbyterian organization was more complicated. Presbyterian missionaries were both members of and responsible to the Korean General Assembly, but the Nevius Plan guarded against the smothering of the church by the mission by separating the two into parallel agencies. Integration of the two, as worked out by the several bodies, involved formation of joint councils or departments of co-operative work, with varying degrees of responsibility to the General Assembly. Through these councils Korean Christians and missionaries together conducted all work that called for co-operation between the Korean church and the churches abroad.

But however the different churches work out the technicalities of co-operation, the Korean church has come of age and the Christian churches of the world have a new partner for their "partnership in mission." With no little pride one Korean church not long ago dispatched its first missionary to America. And who is to say that Korea was not qualified to send him, or that America does not need him.

If there is any doubt, let Americans remember the story of In-Ho Oh. In Korea he was a Christian, active and cheerful in the three-hundred-member Yong Do Presbyterian Church for refugees in Pusan. In America he was murdered. All he did was go to the corner near the University of Pennsylvania, where he was studying, to mail a letter home to Pusan. Just outside his door he was set upon by a gang of eleven teen-age hoodlums. They beat and kicked him into unconsciousness. Then they ran. Ten minutes after police carried Oh into the hospital, he died. This was in Philadelphia, the City of Brotherly Love.

At the funeral, Mayor Dilworth began to say, "It's a horrible thing that this could happen in our city. . . ." Then, overcome with emotion, he could go no farther.

Oh's parents in Korea were stunned. But out of their grief they wrote a letter to the city of Philadelphia:

"We hope you can spare a piece of land in your country and bury our boy there," they wrote, "for your land is part of the homeland of Christians. Thus we will remember your people, and you remember our people, and both you and we will sense more vitally an obligation for better guidance of juvenile delinquents whose souls are unsaved and whose human nature is paralyzed. We hope in this way to make his tomb a monument which will call attention of people to this cause."

As for the boys who had killed their son, Mr. and Mrs. Oh felt no bitterness. Give them "the most lenient treatment possible" under your laws, they wrote, and let us as a Korean Christian family turn our sorrow "into Christian purpose" by giving a little of what we have to start a fund for a ministry to delinquent boys in your city.

Americans later called this letter an "Epistle from the Koreans," and that is what it was: Korean Christians speaking in love to areas of American life still untouched by the gospel. It is a symbol of today's new dimension in Christian mission.

5 | PRESSURES ON THE CHURCH

Nᴏᴛ ᴀʟʟ ᴡᴀꜱ ɢʀᴏᴡᴛʜ ᴀɴᴅ ᴘʀᴏɢʀᴇꜱꜱ ɪɴ ᴛʜᴇ
Korean church during the years of its rising. There were times
when the Rising Sun of Japan seemed to eclipse the Risen
Christ. There were times when waves of bugle blowing Communists threatened to add all of South Korea's twenty million
people to the eight hundred million already behind the Curtain. And there were times when the Korean church's own
worst enemy was itself.

Japanese Persecution

"They are propagating Christianity in Korea, but pay no
attention to the interests of Japan, the sovereign of Korea,"
exclaimed an angry Japanese spokesman, Mr. Midoru Komatsu. "While engaged in Christian propaganda work, the American Missionaries run schools and diffuse foreign political
and social ideas among the half-civilized people. The principle of liberty is recklessly advocated among them. . . . As a
result some Korean converts to Christianity are so senseless

66

as to have recourse to radical action. . . . Under the mask of Christianity . . . [they] have created the present disturbances." Komatsu's words were typical of an attitude on the part of Korea's Japanese conquerors that proved to be the first powerful check on the progress of the Korean church.

Japan had moved swiftly after her victory over China in 1895 to consolidate her hold on Korea. Only Russia contested her claims, but Russia was brushed aside in the Russo-Japanese War of 1904-05. In 1910 the five hundred-year-old Yi dynasty bowed to the inevitable and four thousand years of freedom came to an end. The annexation was a humiliating blow to a proud and sensitive people. Dr. James S. Gale tells of a young man, suspected of dangerous independent sentiments, who was arrested by Japanese police. "I am in prison," he wrote to his father. "Be patient, my son," the father answered, "we are all in prison."

Japan's militant colonizers were distrustful of the church from the start, and not without reason. Nationalist sentiments boiled in Christian circles, though missionaries counseled moderation and sought to avoid involvement in political problems. Harassments of the church became increasingly frequent. A Japanese pastor, after a trip to Korea, protested the injustices he noted. "A company of Japanese soldiers," he wrote, "burnt down a Christian church from a mere fit of passion. On another occasion a party of soldiers entered a church during a prayer meeting and demanded lodging. When asked to wait till the end of the service, they drove out the congregation at the end of bayonets, and occupied the church for the night."

World attention, however, was not aroused to the situation

until the notorious Conspiracy Case of 1912. A hundred and twenty-three Koreans were suddenly arrested and charged with a fantastic plot to assassinate the Japanese governor-general, Count Terauchi, as he passed through Pyongyang. Ninety-eight of the arrested men were Christians, among them the most prominent Korean Christian in the country at the time, Baron Tchi-Ho Yoon. It was at Yoon's invitation, it will be remembered, that Southern Methodists first entered Korea. At the time of his arrest he was vice-president of the Korean Y.M.C.A. and principal of a Methodist academy in Kaesong.

Some of the charges brought against the accused were ridiculous. Chin-Hyong Kiel, son of Korea's best-known evangelist, the Rev. Sun-Chu Kiel of Pyongyang, and brother of Dr. Greenfield Kiel, the present general secretary of the Korean National Christian Council, was charged with singing a dangerously inflammatory anti-Japanese song at a secret meeting. The "secret meeting" was a party, and the song was "Way Down Upon the Swanee River." Two missionaries, the Rev. George S. McCune and Dr. S. A. Moffett, though not arrested, were publicly accused of stirring up students to attack and of packing guns for the plotters in orange crates, yet Dr. Moffett was not even in the country at the time of the alleged crime. Excruciating torture was used to wring confessions from the prisoners. C. H. Kiel never recovered from the treatment he received. Finally, though all of the men publicly repudiated their forced confessions in open court, six were found guilty and imprisoned, among them Baron Yoon. The lesson was not lost on Korea's non-Christians. It was no longer quite so popular to become a Christian.

More subtle pressures were also brought to bear against the church; the government began to strangle it with red tape. Medical regulations in 1913 made it increasingly difficult for missionary physicians to obtain licenses to practice in Korea. New regulations in 1915 brought all religions under bureaucratic controls, and voluminous reports were demanded on the teachings, methods of propagation, and qualifications of ministers and preachers. Censorship was rigid. Most serious of all, Christian schools were presented with a ten-year deadline to meet new requirements forbidding the teaching of religion as a curricular subject. To anxious Christians it seemed that the Bible, central in the whole structure of the church's school system, was about to be forced out of the schools.

Moreover, as enforced secularization began to deprive the Christian schools of their distinctive religious values, they were challenged and eclipsed in academic prestige by the rise of the government educational system. In 1910 Korea had more students in Christian schools than in public schools, but by 1918 the number of students in government schools had outstripped the students in Christian schools three to one.

But "when a people saturated in the Bible comes into touch with tyranny," wrote a visiting British correspondent in Korea, "either one of two things happens, the people are exterminated or tyranny ceases." In Korea in 1919 it appeared to most observers that the people were courting extermination. They arose in a massive nonviolent demonstration for freedom to which Japanese militarists responded with a brutality that shocked the world. Korea's Christians had insisted on non-violence as the price of their participation in the movement, so on March 1, as the people rose against their oppressors, they marched under instructions that read: "Whatever you do, do not insult the Japanese; do not throw stones; do not hit with your fists, for these are the acts of barbarians."

It was naive; it was hopeless; it was Christian; and since fifteen of the thirty-three signers of the Declaration of Independence were Christians, the church was particularly vulnerable to retaliation. Nearly every Christian pastor in Seoul was jailed. Police with drawn swords rushed the nonviolent demonstrators. When Christian nurses from Severance Hospital hurried out to bind up the wounds of the injured, they were arrested too. Soldiers stopped passers-by and asked, "Are you Christian?" If they answered "Yes," they were beaten. If they answered "No," they were released. In rural areas, the brutality was unspeakable.

If Japan's militarists, who had strangled Christian growth in Korea by ten years of pressure, now hoped that they could finish it off with a show of terror, they dangerously miscalculated both their own strength and the resilient courage of Korea's Christians. The year 1919 did not wipe out the church; it ushered it into a new period of growth.

Part of the reason for this change was that the demonstrations purged Korea's soul of ten years of shame and recovered for the nation its self-respect. Japan's brutal persecution of Christians for their share in the independence movement, far from discrediting them, had precisely the opposite effect. It spotlighted them as heroes and martyrs for the whole country. To be a Christian was to be a patriot again.

Outraged world opinion brought an abrupt halt to Japan's

suppression of the independence movement. "No neutrality for brutality," said the missionaries, openly appealing for outside support for the oppressed Koreans. The Federation of Churches in Japan sent the secretary of the mission board of the Japanese Methodist Church to appraise the situation. His report was a stinging rebuke to his own country. In brief, he accused Japan of crippling Koreans educationally; systematically forcing Korean farmers off the land; military tyranny; and cultural annihilation of all things Korean. In conclusion he called for a campaign to raise money among Japanese Christians for the Koreans and their churches.

As a result of world pressures the Japanese government instituted a new and gentler Korea policy, and Christians leaped to take advantage of it within the church. Evangelistic campaigns were vigorously promoted, notably the Methodist Centenary, celebrating one hundred years of American Methodist missions. Its leader was the Rev. J. S. Ryang, who later became the first Korean Methodist bishop. Christian schools won a reprieve and pressed forward. In 1923, two years before the deadline that would have forced the Bible out of the curriculum, an agreement was negotiated, permitting private schools that succeeded in meeting high government educational standards to be "designated" as the equivalent of government recognized schools but retaining the right to teach religion.

New difficulties, however, soon beset the church, and the years from 1925 to 1929 saw another decline in growth. The most obvious factor causing the decline seemed to be an economic depression, world-wide in its effects, but aggravated in Korea by Japan's colonial policies. Energetic and resourceful, the Japanese undeniably improved Korea spectacularly, but they impoverished the Koreans. Eight out of every ten Koreans, according to the census of 1928, depended upon farming for a living, but paddy field by paddy field, Korea's emerald green rice lands were slipping into the hands of the Japanese. And taxes levied against the hard pressed Koreans increased threefold in nine years.

The effect of the depression upon a self-supporting church was to starve it of fulltime paid leadership. A 1927 study of church giving in Korea concluded that the church was paying only half enough toward an adequate income for its church workers. The principle of self-support, said critics of the Nevius Plan, had arbitrarily frozen the church at too low a level of development, intellectually and culturally. It simply didn't have the resources to train and retain qualified leadership.

The problems of economic depression soon faded before a far more serious threat, a revival of Japanese militarism. In the early 1930's Japanese nationalists lifted their eyes to the Chinese mainland and began to dream of continental conquest. But to conquer a continent, as Japan knew and as others sometimes forget, the nation needed more than an army; it needed a faith. And unfortunately, even a false faith will do, as the Communists have discovered. This false faith the militarists had ready-made for them in Shinto, which is popularly known as the worship of the Japanese Emperor as the divine descendant of Amaterasu, the sun-goddess. To bind the whole Empire into a fighting, fanatic force for world conquest, Japan proceeded to try to force this faith on all her people—even the Koreans. Shinto shrines began to

72

appear in every town. Government schools were ordered out en masse to Shinto ceremonies.

Private schools at first were exempted from these ceremonies, but in the fall of 1935 the missionary principals of two Christian schools in Pyongyang were invited to a conference of educational leaders. As the conference opened, reports Dr. Allen D. Clark in his *History of the Korean Church*, which gives the best summary of the Shrine Question, the governor rose and said, "Before we take up the agenda we will all go by car to the new Shinto Shrine and worship." The missionaries objected. "Your honor," said Dr. George S. McCune, president of Union Christian College (Soongsil), "[we] must ask you to excuse us . . . it is impossible for us, as Christians, to take part in such ceremonies." McCune was angrily ordered home and given sixty days to reconsider or lose his permit to teach.

Seriously disturbed, the missionaries then called a meeting of the pastors in the city and asked for advice. All but one of the pastors urged them to stand by their convictions. "We know that the worship of deified spirits at the shrines is contrary to God's commandments," said the pastors' spokesman. "We also know that terrible pressure will be put on the Korean church, which many of us will not be able to withstand. Therefore we ask you missionaries today, while we are able to speak, to protect the faith of the church, no matter what happens." Then, sewing the garments of faith around them, the pastors went out to face the future, and in that future not all retained the faith.

Pressures mounted from reasoned pleadings to savage violence. Dr. McCune was driven from the country in six months. An attempt to reach a compromise understanding between church and government failed. It had been hoped that a distinction might be made between two different types of Shinto ceremonies: specifically religious ceremonies, on the one hand, and national patriotic observances, on the other. But such a distinction was not readily maintained.

Pressure fell first on the schools. Some Christian schools closed rather than compromise. Others stayed open, fearing that if they closed they would only be driving their students into government schools beyond all help from Christian advisers. Then pressure fell on the churches. Police came to one presbytery and said, "You already worship three Gods, Father, Son, and Holy Ghost. All we ask you to do is add a fourth, the Emperor. Why balk at such a little thing?"

Japanese church leaders urged the Koreans to accept a workable compromise. "Treat the ceremonies as only patriotic, like saluting the flag," they urged. "Let that ease your consciences. But don't insist on a government denial of their religious nature." To some this seemed a reasonable solution of the problem.

The matter reached its climax at the 1938 meeting of the Presbyterian General Assembly. All four hundred delegates, missionaries as well as Koreans, were called to local police stations before being allowed to leave for the Assembly. Police bluntly told them that the Assembly must pass an action approving Shrine worship. No debate and no negative votes would be permitted. When some delegates thereupon determined to absent themselves from the meeting, they were sent up under police escort. The Assembly finally approved the shrine resolution, without allowing debate or a negative vote. This action gave the police a tool with which to destroy all resistance throughout the church.

After Pearl Harbor, when all missionaries had been forced from the country, an ardent Shintoist and rabid militarist was made governor general of Korea. In 1943 he abruptly suppressed three Korean denominations—the Holiness Church (established by the Oriental Missionary Society), the Seventh-day Adventists, and Fenwick's East Asia Christian Church (Baptist)—because of their emphasis on the Second Coming. The return of Christ implied, he believed, an end to the Japanese Empire. Pastors were arrested and tortured for failure to attend Shinto ceremonies. The number of Christians who suffered imprisonment for their faith is estimated at about three thousand, of whom some fifty paid the price of martyrdom. Uncounted numbers "abandoned the visible church in order to maintain the highest standards of the invisible church," escaping to mountain villages, or worshiping only in private.

About a month before the end of the war the final blow was delivered. All denominational distinctions were ordered abolished, and all the churches were squeezed into one tightly controlled organization, the united "Korean Christian Church of Japanese Christianity." Christians were shocked when a Shinto priest led a procession of Christian pastors to the Han River for the opening ceremony of purification. It was a bizarre and frightening spectacle, explaining, perhaps, some of the passion of later church controversies over collaboration and throwing light on Korean Christianity's present resistance to proposals for church union.

A few days after this forced union large numbers of church

leaders were arrested, including even some of those who had co-operated with the government. On the day of the Japanese surrender, they were released. Only later was it discovered that their execution had been ordered for August 18. The surrender was August 15. Japan's early capitulation after the Hiroshima bombing saved more than American and Japanese lives.

But contrary to all their expectations, liberation, so deliriously greeted by Korean Christians, only exposed them to deadlier peril. Communists in the north, and schisms in the south confronted the church with unexpected danger.

Communist Pressures

Only for a few short months were Christians in the north able to rejoice in freedom, but in those months they proceeded to reorganize their churches. Presbyterians formed a temporary northern General Assembly, pending reunion with the churches of the south from whom they had been cut off by the arbitrary division of the country at the 38th parallel. A country-wide Freedom Memorial Evangelistic campaign was launched. The Presbyterian Theological Seminary in Pyongyang, closed in protest against Shrine worship, was reopened, and when Dr. W. N. Blair, the only missionary allowed briefly back into Communist North Korea, visited it in April, 1947, he found 164 students in attendance.

But communism is a more constrictive totalitarianism than Japanese militarism ever had been. There were three stages of the Communists' attack on religion as an organized force. First, in 1946, they broke Christian attempts to organize politically for freedom. The Rev. Kyung-Chik Han's Social

Democratic party was smashed in the far north, at Sinuiju. In Pyongyang the Rev. Hwa-Sik Kim's Christian Liberal party was likewise brutally suppressed, and Mr. Kim with forty of his colleagues died in prison or disappeared.

Next the Communists tried to enslave the church. They organized a puppet Christian League to bully the church into support of the Communist regime, and when Christians responded by boycotting the League, the Communists made membership in the League mandatory for all church officers. But by 1950, though the Methodist and Presbyterian seminaries had been forcibly combined into one "Christian Seminary," the League had proved itself so much a failure that the Communists despaired of ever winning control of the church and moved instead to wipe it out. This was the third and final stage of their religious policy: extermination. Church buildings were confiscated and leaders were imprisoned and, as the Korean war progressed, wherever Communist control was threatened by allied advances, the retreating Communists invariably massacred the Christians to prevent their liberation. How many perished in this way is not known, even estimates of the number of Protestant ministers murdered by the Communists vary, but there were probably over four hundred who were killed.

At the end of 1950, as the United Nations troops fought across the 38th parallel and made their victorious way to the icy Yalu, the Communists lost control of North Korea. Many thought that after five years of Communist persecution there would be no North Korean church left, for a modern dictatorship can wipe out all organized resistance in such a length of time. But as the Communist capital fell, a high ranking American general was flown in from Tokyo. He entered Pyongyang on a Sunday and found the streets choked with Koreans. "A welcoming demonstration?" he asked an aide. "No," replied the officer. "They tell me those are Christians going to church."

But the Curtain fell again. Chinese troops moved across the Yalu in December, 1950, and the U.N. forces, caught by surprise, regrouped, retreated, and their retreat came perilously close to being a rout. Millions of North Koreans chose to flee south with the retreating U.N. troops rather than stay to live once more under the Communists. Five years had forever destroyed any illusions they might have had about a better life under the leadership of the Party. And so they fled, with or without their belongings. Among them were as many of North Korea's Christians as were able to move.

As the Red armies approached one town on the east coast, Korean Christians besieged a missionary turned chaplain, Harold Voelkel. "Our lives and our children's lives are in your hands. Take us with you," they said in simple trust. But what could the chaplain do? It was all the army could do to evacuate its own. It had no time for refugees. At the last moment, however, an overworked Chief of Staff granted permission for three thousand Koreans to be given army transportation out of the encircled city of Hamhung, and the chaplain raced through the dark streets of the falling city to gather them in.

In one little Holiness church the congregation had gathered to meet death together. All hope of escape gone, they had decided to come together and pray on their knees in God's house as they waited for the Communists to return.

"Lord, send us a Moses to deliver us out of bondage," the leader prayed as the people wept. At that moment the chaplain's Korean aide opened the door, took in the situation at a glance, and with a Korean's love of the dramatic, pointed to Harold Voelkel and shouted, "Moses has come!" And the congregation went with him, and crossed the sea in safety, and were free. Four and a half million refugees fled into South Korea in those few months—all things lost, but freedom gained.

There are not many Christians left in North Korea now. All who could, escaped. "Do you ever see Christians going to church back there across the line?" a defector was asked. This was in 1960, and such defections were and are rare. But occasionally a man, like this reporter, manages to slip across at the armistice headquarters in Panmunjom. The defector thought for a moment before answering the question, "No. There are some churches still standing," he said, "but they are used by the Communists now. I don't know of any Sunday services." "Don't you even hear any church bells ring on Sunday?" he was asked. "No," he replied, "they don't ring any more."

The church bells are silent, and the churches are empty, but it is not true to say that there are no Christians there. A Swiss member of the neutral nations truce team tells of an evening when the team was invited to a party given by Communists in Kaesong, which is across the 38th parallel. As the United Nations representatives drove through the streets of the Communist city, there suddenly floated out from an open window the sound of a voice singing. The Korean words were unknown to the Swiss member but he recognized the hymn—

"Jesus Loves Me." Someone wanted the truce team to know that there are Christians still in North Korea.

Division in the South

While Christians in the Communist north, silent and scattered but still surviving, were proving once again the old truth that "religion is like a nail; the harder you hit it the deeper you drive it in," Christians in the south were discovering that freedom and power and prosperity can sometimes pose greater problems for the church than persecution.

Statistically the church was flowering. Congregations overflowed the churches, and the churches overflowed the towns —tent churches, wooden churches, mud churches, churches made of flattened beer cans, churches made of brick, and even cathedral-like churches of polished stone. But not always was everything well within the church. "The trouble with Seoul," more than one Korean has said in recent years, "is that it has too many automoblies, too many tea houses, and too many churches." They are not bitter so much as disappointed, these non-Christian Koreans when they talk about the church. For years, although they had never joined the church, most of them had respected it and appreciated its brave part in the long Korean fight for liberty. They even turned to it for leadership. When the Republic of Korea chose its first president and first national assembly in 1948, the president, and most of his cabinet, and 25 per cent of the assembly were Christian—and that in a country not yet 7 per cent Christian. But now with freedom won, and the whole nation looking to the church for guidance into freedom, the church began to fall apart.

Korea – Land of the Morning Calm

Timeless . . .

. . . yet changing

sometimes violently – as by revolution

from within .

Police action against student demonstrators helped to spark the overthrow of the Rhee government in 1960

. . . or by war from without

Worker sifts through debris for salvage after marching and counter-
marching armies had reduced Seoul to rubble during the Korea War

Change comes quietly, too, in the heart of a man . .

. . . a change that is in itself changeless

Still the past remains . . .

. . . in old ways of doing things

Former Queen Yoonbi, wearing her robes of state for the first time in the half century since the Japanese overthrew the Yi Dynasty, emerges from her seclusion to welcome visitors to the newly restored royal residence

The past lingers . . .

One of Korea's million and a half Buddhists, this nun is associated with the country's most famous temple, the Hae In Sa, located in the mountains near Taegu

. . . in the people

Many travellers to the city stop to pay their respects to the battered Andong Buddha, believed to be well over a thousand years old

Sometimes past and present meet . . .

Almost lost in the modern city, Seoul's historic Great South Gate is a rare example of early Yi Dynasty (1392-1910) architecture

Rice offering is collected from bags hung on wall by church members who have tithed their family food supply, day by day, meal by meal

The past was shaped by the
unchanging
mountains . . .

. . . by the
rushing rivers

. . . by the tireless sea

But the "unchanging" changes

rivers become power plants

villages become cities

Bible school student evangelizes outside
one of Korea's oldest Confucian villages

children

become leaders

The ROK army joins civilians to pave a much needed highway

farmers become . . .

. . . city workers

and the Hermit Kingdom becomes
a part of the Family of Nations

**Korean manufactured telephone equipment undergoes
rigid inspection before being shipped out to market**

Six pointed hat denotes standing of Confucian scholar
who is custodian of ancestral records in his village

But timelessness can never be lost . . .

It endures . . .

"The ferocious tiger
with grinding teeth—who
would dare to confront him?
Grievous times bring forth
the old Yellow Lord
of the Eastern seas.
Who today recognizes
among the swaggerers
and the perverse,
these same tigers?"

(Painting and poem by
Sajong Sin, 1707-1768)

. . . creatively

An outstanding example of ceramic art, the Thousand Crane Vase is a black and white incised celadon typical of the distinguished 12th century Koryu Dynasty

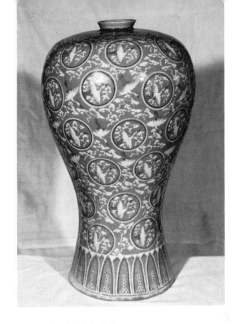

One of best preserved examples of Buddhist stone work, the Pul Guk Sa temple in Kyungju dates from the Silla Dynasty, about A.D. 800

... *historically*

A devil's post is an important factor in the life of many fishing villages where shamanist practices are still strongly entrenched

The world's first movable type, on carved wooden blocks now preserved at Hae In Sa temple, predates Gutenberg by five hundred years and records the most complete set of Buddhist writings extant

. . . in the inventions of a people

The oldest observatory in the Far East was built in Korea's ancient capital of Kyunju in the 7th century

. . . in the songs they sing

Pilgrims to the cave temple at Sokuram offer prayers to Buddha beneath bas reliefs that are noteworthy for the evidences they show of Semitic and Hellenic influence

... in the way they worship

Ancient animistic practices linger in the mountain areas where travellers propitiate the demons by tossing prayer stones beneath a spirit tree

Timeless as suffering

Changing as politics

Junta soldier guards thoroughfare in Seoul from the top of Korean National Christian Council building during May 1961 *coup d'état*

Old as Buddha

The Miryok or Messiah Buddha, of undetermined age and origin, now stands on the ruins of an old temple outside of Chungju

New as hope

Wedding of fourth generation Christian bride attracts too many guests for indoor ceremony

Korea . . .

The original of this photograph of pioneer missionaries J. S. Gale and S. A. Moffett was discovered in Korean government archives. Just as the picture of these Westerners became an enduring fragment of Korean records so has the Christian faith become a bright pattern in the timeless-changing culture of the Land of the Morning Calm.

Picture story by Bette Virginia Reed

It was not the breakup of the synthetic united church, the Korean Christian Church formed during the Japanese occupation, that was disturbing. That was expected. Some of its compromised leaders forlornly tried to hold it together, but it soon fell apart and few mourned its passing. The old, familiar denominations were quickly reorganized. As one leader put it, "Having been pushed into a forced marriage, we were homesick for our family home. So we have decided to go back home for a visit, but fully intend to return to our marriage relationship voluntarily in the near future."

So much for the good intentions. Once back home, though, the families began to quarrel, as families do, which is normal enough in normal times, but the times were not normal. Years of struggle against outside enemies had so drained the people emotionally and physically that they no longer had the strength and the love to forgive and forget after a family quarrel. What would have been minor irritations in normal times now were magnified into major issues, and quarrels led straight to divorce.

Methodist divisions, providentially, have all been healed. In February, 1946, a group of leaders who had resisted Shinto compromises reopened the Methodist Theological Seminary in Seoul, condemned the "Japanized" united church, and prepared to reconstitute the Korean Methodist Church. But when the united church fell apart, and the Methodist Church actually did reorganize, this group found itself in the minority and was bypassed in the elections as the majority proceeded to forgive and elect to office some who had been guilty of wartime collaboration. Self-righteous and hurt, the minority group withdrew to form the Rehabilitated Methodist Church—a schism that was bridged three years later.

A second Methodist schism, although of longer duration, was even more minor, involving as it did a dispute over the legality of an emergency election of a bishop in the 1950 invasion crisis. Bishop Yoon-Soon Kim had been captured and killed by the Communists. An emergency session of the Conference in Pusan on Nov. 1, 1950, elected the Rev. Hyungi Lew as Bishop to succeed the martyred leader. A small group, however, challenged the constitutionality of the action and withdrew to form the Constitutional Methodist Church. The schism ended in 1959.

Far more serious, and immeasurably more damaging to Protestant prestige and evangelistic effectiveness and even perhaps to the faith of some believers, were the schisms that tore the Presbyterian Church in Korea into four jagged pieces, not to mention some smaller fragments.

In 1951 the Koryu Presbyterian Church seceded from the Presbyterian Church in Korea, charging that the parent body was too liberal, too ecumenical, and too tainted with Shinto collaborationism. Ministers guilty of compromise had been censured by the General Assembly and removed from their pulpits for two months of penance and repentance, but this did not satisfy the purists. Collaborators, they said, are permanently unfit for church leadership, no matter how they repent. To this local issue was added an imported divisive factor. The dissidents were supported by fundamentalist mission bodies related to the Orthodox and Bible Presbyterian schisms in America, which were all too eager to accuse other Presbyterians of liberalism.

By way of contrast, the Presbyterian Church in the Republic of Korea separated from the parent body in 1954, charging that it was too conservative. Technically the issue in dispute was the authority of the General Assembly over two Presbyterian theological seminaries, one considered conservative, and the other (now called the Hankuk Seminary) charged with being liberal. In the opinion of the General Assembly, the rivalry between these two seminaries was dividing the church. It therefore ordered both of them to close and proposed to open one new seminary under its own authority in order to unite the church. But the Hankuk Seminary, fearing the conservative majority in the assembly, refused to obey and its leaders were excommunicated, organizing themselves into the Presbyterian Church in the R.O.K. as distinct from the Presbyterian Church in Korea. They are in close fellowship with the United Church of Canada.

In 1959 occurred the most virulent schism of all. Presbyterians watched in anguish as the Presbyterian Church in Korea (Old Assembly), still one of the largest Christian bodies in Asia despite its earlier divisions, split again into two fighting factions and two rival assemblies. The division was caused by a minority clique of dissidents who preferred to split the church than remain and face charges of ethical misconduct. They were enthusiastically supported by that "apostle of discord," Dr. Carl McIntyre, a professional schismatic who has three times split his own church in America. Fighting and shouting, the dissidents withdrew to form the Anti-Ecumenical Assembly that accused missionaries and Korean Christian leaders alike of heresy, pro-communism, and ecclesiastical vaticanism. An attempt by this group to join forces with the earlier fundamentalist schism (the Koryu Presbyterian Church) in a Reunited Anti-Ecumenical Assembly has been partially successful, but the uneasy union has unfortunately also further splintered the right-wing groups.

Presbyterianism in Korea, therefore, is now a confusing mosaic of the following denominations (with a rough guess as to the total number of adherents in each body):

Presbyterian Church in Korea	375,000
Reunited Anti-Ecumenical Assembly (1951 and 1959 schisms)	220,000
Presbyterian Church in the R.O.K. (1954 schism)	114,000
Continuing Koryu Presbyterian Church (1951 schism)	66,000

Divisions have also recently occurred in the Holiness Church between ecumenical and anti-ecumenical factions, and in the Baptist Churches between congregations that trace back to Fenwick's Church of Christ in Corea and congregations loyal to the newer Baptist missions.

A related problem is the disturbing rise of a number of semi-Christian sects, largest and most notorious of which is the Olive Tree Church. Its leader is a one-time manufacturer, evangelist, and faith-healer, Tae-Sun Park (Tae Seon Bak), who grandly claims that he is one of the Olive Trees foretold in the Book of Revelation (11:4). In his veins, he shouts, flows the very blood of Jesus Christ. The merest touch of his bath water will cure disease, declare his followers. He has been expelled by the Presbyterian Church and jailed by the Korean government on proved charges of fraud, but nothing shakes the faith of his credulous followers, who may number as high as a hundred thousand. Like a Korean Father Divine, Park has built for them a "heavenly village" of six hundred modern houses near Seoul, supported partly by the life savings of the faithful who must turn over all their worldly possessions to the church, and partly by ten small but well-organized factories.

Protestants are hurt and bewildered at the spectacle of so much division in so short a time in a church signally blessed by the marks of growth and spiritual strength. Why, after sixty-five years of harmony and co-operation in the great task of winning Korea for Christ, have the churches been devastated by a decade of division?

Some blame it on the war. There is no question that the horrors of the Korean war, following so closely upon the persecutions of World War II, left Korea's Christians nervously and physically exhausted, introverted spiritually by their attempts to escape compromise, and isolated intellectually from developments in the churches of other lands. Others say that the reasons for division are to be found in what they claim are built-in weaknesses in the fabric of Korean Christianity—legalism, over-literal biblicism, and a doctrinaire creedalism that exalts orthodoxy at the expense of ethics. Not all agree with this criticism, but anyone familiar with the Korean church will recall extreme examples, fortunately not typical, of tendencies in this direction, such as the case of a Bible institute dean who shrugged when students were reported for cheating but swiftly expelled two girls who cut and curled their hair.

Some blame the West for the major factors contributing to the divisions. It is frequently charged that the root of the

117

trouble was the foreign dollar, whether as the root of controversy over available funds or as a subsidy maintaining the divisions that developed. Western ecumenical rivalries were a further troubling element as the World Council of Churches, the National Association of Evangelicals, and Dr. McIntyre's belligerent little International Council of Christian Churches competed for recognition in Korea. Western missions in Korea, it is also asserted, had too much of a narrow oneness in their theological emphases, and had failed to prepare Korea for the sharp impact of new ideas and the criticism of more liberal interpretations of the Christian faith. On the other hand, still others blame the divisions not on the West, but on national Korean character traits—fierce regional loyalties, factionalisms that are as old as Korea's royal dynasties, and a national fondness for political maneuvering that is the despair of the country's best friends.

Whatever the complex of reasons may have been for the shattering fragmentation of the denominations in Korea, it ill becomes Christians in a country that has just spawned its own newest schism, the No-Television Baptist Church in eastern Kentucky, to sit in judgment on division in Korea. Nor should Western churches have been quite so surprised at the tragic developments. After all, division after persecution is a pattern of Donatist schism almost as old as the Christian church itself.

The Church Survives

"Don't be too discouraged about our fighting," said the amiable general secretary of the Korean Bible Society, the Rev. Yong-Bin Im, at a recent luncheon in New York. "After all, if children in the family never fight, you know they must be sick. Fighting is a sign that they are alive."

The church in Korea is alive, there is no doubt about that. Even in the midst of division it continues to grow. A five year program to establish five hundred new congregations is so far from being crippled by schism in the church that it is already ahead of schedule at the end of three years. "Give a seminary student a tent," said a Christian leader in Korea, "and in six months he will have a self-supporting congregation."

Not even a revolution could stem the growth of the church. When the Syngman Rhee regime was toppled by student uprisings in April, 1960, it was anticipated that although Roman Catholic political influence might rise with the election as prime minister of Dr. John Chang, a devout Catholic layman, Protestant prestige would decline, for Protestantism had been associated in the minds of many with the fortunes of Rhee, a Methodist. But to the contrary, in the Second Republic Protestants were as active and omnipresent as ever. The president of the Second Republic, Po-Sun Yoon, was a Presbyterian elder. Dr. George Paik, a Presbyterian minister who resigned after fourteen years of distinguished service as president of Yonsei University to run for political office, was overwhelmingly elected to the House of Councillors (the Korean senate) and was later chosen president of that body. The Foreign Minister and the Education Minister were both Methodists, and the Minister of Commerce and Industry was a Presbyterian elder.

It is true that the coup d'état of May, 1961, which overthrew the Second Republic and established a military government, may lead to diminishing Christian participation in government. The leader of the junta, General Chung-Hee Park, became the first non-Christian to head the government of Korea since independence. He had no religious affiliation. Christian influence, however, did continue to be present in government circles. Dr. Po-Sun Yoon was kept on as president of the Republic, and at least two members of the new cabinet were Christians. No government restrictions were placed upon the church, and, although nonreligious gatherings of any kind had to have a government permit to convene, church services were completely free of control.

As long as Korea produces Christians like the Rev. Yang-Won Son, neither persecution nor war nor division caused by schism shall ever destroy the Korean church. Pastor Son was the minister of a church near the Southern Presbyterian center of Soonchun. He was a mild, little man—less than five feet tall—whose two great joys in life were his two sons, Tong-In and Tong-Sin. During the war Tong-In, like his father, had refused to worship at the Shinto shrines and had been thrown out of school by the Japanese. After the war, at twenty-four years of age, he went back to high school, where he was elected president of the campus Y.M.C.A. But in October, 1948, a wild Communist uprising swept through his part of South Korea, and Communist youths seized the school in a reign of terror. A nineteen-year-old Communist leveled a pistol at Tong-In and ordered him to renounce his Christian faith. But Tong-In only pleaded with him to turn Christian himself and try the Christian way of love. Tong-Sin, the younger brother, rushed up to save him.

"Shoot me," he shouted, "and let my brother live."

"No," cried Tong-In, "I am the elder. I am the one who should die. Shoot me."

The Communist shot them both, and when Pastor Son was brought to see the bodies, all he said was, "Their shining faces are as lovely as flowers."

Two days later the uprising was smashed and the murderer of the two boys was caught and brought to trial. Pastor Son found him with his hands tied behind his back, about to be condemned to death. He went to the military commander. "No amount of punishment will bring back my two sons," he said, "so what is to be gained by this? Let me, instead, take the boy and make a Christian of him, so that he can do the work in the world that Tong-In and Tong-Sin left undone."

Stunned at first by the proposal, the authorities reluctantly consented to release the young man into the custody of the father of the boys he had killed, and Pastor Son took him home. The boy's own parents were overcome with gratitude. "Let us feed and clothe your daughter, in return," they offered. But the pastor's sixteen-year-old daughter was hesitant. She did not relish the prospect of living with the parents of her brothers' murderer. Only after talking it over with her father, who told her, "It is the best Christian witness you could make," did she agree.

Retold in this way it all sounds deceptively simple, perhaps. But it was not simple, and it was not easy. It took love, so much love, that Koreans call the now deceased Pastor Son, "the apostle of love."

6 | THE CHURCH IN SOCIETY

THERE IS ONLY ONE MOUNTAIN IN KOREA NAMED for a foreigner. Mt. Lutz near Taejon bears the name of a missionary, and honors Dr. Dexter N. Lutz, an agriculturist. It stands wide and high above the narrow valleys—a symbol of Christianity's broad impact on every phase of Korean life and thought.

No national problem or interest has been considered beyond the scope of Christian care and concern. For although the church has been built most surely in the realm of the spirit, if there had been no visible, concrete demonstration of Christian compassion and involvement in the daily problems and physical needs of the people, the church might not have been built at all. Medical missionary Horace Allen, who later headed the United States legation in Korea, made possible Korea's first railroad, her first waterworks, her first city lighting, her first streetcars, and her first modern mine—as well as her first hospital.

It was medicine, not preaching, that opened Korea to the Protestant church. It was education, not evangelism, that first commended it to the authorities. Some of the earliest criticism of the pioneer missionaries, in fact, centered about their interest in other than strictly religious matters. When Underwood imported kerosene and agricultural implements, and Moffett and Lee organized a timber concession on the Yalu, and Swallen brought in Korea's first apple trees and started an orchard in Wonsan, European and American traders protested. Such activities were beyond the province of the missionaries, the traders cried. It was not fair for them to use their knowledge and contacts in commercial enterprises, particularly since the missionaries did not do it for personal gain but rather to teach Koreans modern business methods.

From the beginning the church in Korea served the people with no less zeal than it preached to them. It rescued from oblivion the Korean phonetic alphabet, one of the best in the world, and used it to open the doors of hope for Korea's gentle, slow-moving, illiterate masses. Appenzeller founded Korea's first modern school for boys, and Mrs. Mary F. Scranton, also a Methodist, the first school for girls. Christians were the first nurses. There was not even a word for nurse in the Korean language until Margaret Edmunds, the Methodist mission's first trained nurse, invented one. Dr. Rosetta Hall started the first school for the blind and Christians were the first to bring healing to those suffering from leprosy.

Christians, too, were the first to work for the deaf. At the Church of Eternal Joy not many months ago, the music of the best choir in Korea soared through the great sanctuary with the sound of angels singing, and when the guest soloist, an American Negro GI sang "There is a Balm in Gilead" a hush fell over the 2,500 worshipers. They spoke no English but they understood with their hearts, and you could have heard a pin drop. But down in the semidarkness of a room below, there was another sound and another congregation singing. As the hymn began, twisting fingers flashed out the words, and the sound was low and distorted. Yet on the faces of the forty or fifty people gathered together there was joy, for here in this Christian church some of Korea's deaf-mutes, who are brutally jeered in the villages, have at last found sympathy and love and a warm welcome, and they rejoice to worship God.

It is the broadness of its compassion and the sincerity of its concern for all people and all of life that makes the Korean church, despite the depressing record of its divisions, still the most revolutionary social and religious force in modern Korea. Christians are people, and conversion has not separated them from the problems of the world about them. Korea's Christians face the same problems as their non-Christian neighbors—rural problems, urban problems, medical and educational problems. But they face them with more hope and humor, with more grit and perseverance and success than non-Christians.

The Rural Christian

Like every other Korean, the Korean Christian lives in an overcrowded land, almost as densely populated as Japan, whose population pressures are well known. There are 232 people per square mile in Korea, very close to Japan's 242. By comparison, the figure for Communist China is only 69. North America offers no comparison at all. United States citizens live a comfortable 19 to the square mile, and across the line to the north there are only 5 Canadians to the square mile. Korea has 115 times as many people per square mile as Canada! Nor do such statistics tell the full story, for Korea's millions live elbow to elbow on only 20 per cent of the land surface—the 20 per cent of the land that is arable. The rest is mountain.

In so overcrowded a land, privacy is an unknown luxury. "I didn't know what privacy was before I went to America, but now it is what I long for most of all," wistfully commented a young girl enrolled at Seoul National University. A Christian and a graduate student, she movingly described some of her problems in readjusting to life in Korea. Psychologically, the greatest problem had been the lack of privacy.

Again, like the majority of their countrymen, Korean Christians live for the most part in the country, not in the cities—though the last few years have seen radical changes in the population pattern. In this the Korean church is unlike many of the other churches of Asia. About 80 per cent of the people of Asia are rural but only 20 per cent of Asia's Christian work is rural. The Korean church, however, is a village church. Until the pattern began to change after the Korean War, an estimated 73 per cent of Korea's Christians were rural, a figure remarkably close to the national population percentage at that time.

The typical Korean family lives in a mud-walled house, twenty feet long and ten feet wide, under a roof of thatched yellow straw. The kitchen is at one end on a lower level, and the whole family usually sleeps in one room at the other end —father, mother, and four children, and probably a mother-in-law, bedded-down on the paper covered floor.

Life is lived to the gentle rhythm of the seasons on the little four acre farm, which is really not much more than a large garden, mostly rice paddies if the farmer can manage it. In the winter the terraced paddies freeze in crystal pools but in the spring they turn to deep rich mud through which the farmer guides his plow, sinking to his thighs as he wades behind the ox. In the summer every blade of rice must be set and transplanted by hand, but as it grows the rice is a cascade of emerald green down the valley, the most beautiful green in the world, set against the yellow squash and the red peppers drying on the straw roof. Then the rice ripens and the emerald turns to gold and the harvest is done, the food gathered in, and winter comes once more.

But all the beauty of the land and the seasons cannot hide the quiet desperation of the farmer's life. He owns four acres, statistically speaking, ten trees, seven-tenths of a pig, and half a cow. That is all. And it is not enough. His total income for the family of six is $491 a year. His living expenses are $497. Taxes are another $20. So every year he falls a little deeper into debt, paying interest charges of 36 per cent a year on his debts, while the land that is his life and his love is slowly slipping out of his hands. If he is a Christian, he worries that there is no money for the Sunday offering, but the family faithfully sets aside a few grains of rice every day, and on Sunday they pour the week's collection into a little cloth bag and take it to church to hang on a nail marked with the family name at the side of the sanctuary.

The farmer owns neither watch nor clock. He reads no newspaper. He owns no books. All of Korea's three hundred small rural libraries together contain only twelve thousand books. There is no electricity, no movies, no radio. The whole family spends only two dollars a year on culture and entertainment, and that is not even enough to subscribe to a newspaper. Already they are wondering how they will ever find the twenty-five dollars for their daughter's wedding.

So it goes, year after year. The farmer works hard, from dawn to dusk, and loses more money every year. One year's crop failure can bring a whole district to the raw edge of starvation. Deforestation and erosion ruin more and more of the precious land with each succeeding year. No one who has ever lived through the "death months," from February to April, in a bad crop year when the rice is gone and the spring barley is not yet in, is ever quite the same again.

But what can the church do about it? Isn't this too vast a problem for a little 7 per cent Christian minority to tackle? Not at all. Only an estimated twenty-seven dollars more a year is needed to switch the average farmer's income from loss to beginnings of profit. And it is at this point that Christian leadership can make a valuable economic contribution. After all, the church pioneered in helping the farmer improve his lot. Dexter Lutz began his work, which led a whole nation to honor him, with apple trees.

Early missionaries like Dr. Wilbur Swallen in the north and Dr. James Adams in the south had brought the first apple trees to Korea, and at their urging Christian farmers here and there began to plant their hills in orchards. Just as they were prospering, an apple tree disease began to spread its blight unchecked from orchard to orchard. Then, providentially, Korean missions received their first scientifically trained agricultural missionary, Dexter Lutz.

"Whether my coming to Korea was in answer to the prayers of these Christians I do not know," Lutz wrote, "but at least this disease offered me my first opportunity." The agriculturist hurried to share his knowledge with the farmers, setting up classes to show them how to save the trees not yet attacked by blight.

Dexter Lutz did not stop with apples. He developed drought resistant grains; urged crop diversification; campaigned tirelessly for reforestation of the barren hills and for scientific enrichment of the soil by crop rotation; and founded *Farmers' Life*, which the Korean church still continues to publish. It is one of the very few magazines that teaches the village farmer new methods to help him in his struggle for existence. Mr. Lutz also helped to create Korea's first college department of agriculture at Union Christian College. He deserves to have a mountain named for him, for by faith he moved mountains.

While missionaries were teaching better agricultural methods, the Y.M.C.A. and Y.W.C.A. were pioneering in village improvement. With the help of volunteers, the Y's taught everything from adult literacy to child raising. They gave guidance in co-operative buying and selling, demonstrated public and private hygiene, and started a credit union movement to save the farmers from falling ever more hopelessly in debt year after year.

Today, despite the Korean government's burgeoning program of agricultural studies and technical assistance, the church is still pioneering in rural Korea. The major center for such pioneering is the Union Christian Service Center in Taejon, an interdenominational project for developing rural leadership and solving rural problems. "When I get discouraged about all the divisions in our church," remarked a Korean leader recently, "I like to remember that we still have Christians like Dr. Min-Soo Pai, quietly and faithfully going about his work as always. When I think of him I take fresh heart for my own work."

Dr. Pai is director of the Union Christian Service Center. What Lutz once did with apples, Dr. Pai may some day do with fish. He suggests that every farm should have a stocked fish pond to provide more meat for the diet and extra income for the purse. Whether this particular experiment proves practical or not, it is typical of the surge of new ideas and fresh experiments that come from the Center.

Two agriculture experts are on the staff of the Center, Dean Schowengerdt, a Methodist missionary, and Paul Kingsbury, a Presbyterian. A new appointee of the United Church of Canada is expected to join them soon. An annual Rural Christian Leaders' Institute and short five-day conferences provide practical training for Christian boys who want to stay on the farm and improve the life of their country villages.

Many Institute students are reporting increased income and improved village conditions. One graduate writes, "Our village contributed twenty bags of rice to a public fund; this contribution and some aid from the Institute and staff were used to install an irrigation pump. A good harvest is now assured every year. Previously rice and barley were the main crops, but now, in addition, vegetables and other crops of high market price are grown. My upland income alone (i.e. from non-rice land) was about one thousand dollars." Compare this with the average farmer's seven-tenths of a pig, half a cow, and $491 annual income.

And lest some worry that stress on better crops for better income will deaden the farmer's spiritual life, listen to this testimony from a graduate, who entered as a non-Christian and found Christ at the Institute. "I have many hardships because my parents and other members of my family are not converted yet. But no matter what comes in my life, I will be one of the cells of the Cross of Christ, as I learned from Dr. Pai. I am determined to evangelize my own village through my life and service to God. . . ."

Thanks to the Christians of Korea, there is more than one kind of hope for the villages today. There is hope for the body and hope for the soul, and the village needs both, as many a villager has discovered. But the difference that Christ makes, in the end, is not really economic. The difference is love. Christian love. It begins with God in Christ; it fills the human heart; it reaches out to others. And to build it into the life of the village is the business of the Korean church.

The City and Its Problems

On a corner, partly sheltered by the empty walls of a war gutted building, two youngsters huddled under a leaky bamboo umbrella. It was a dark, rainy afternoon in the dingiest part of town. Water poured down the muddy alleys between canvas covered shacks made of cardboard cartons or straw bags that sagged crazily in the rain. The better ones had roofs of flattened beer cans, but these leaked almost as badly as the others. One of the two boys under the umbrella was a beggar boy; the other was singing at the top of his voice, oblivious to the rain, the dirt, and the squalor all about him, but his song seemed strangely out of place. It was "This Is My Father's World."

It takes a very young Christian, sometimes, to see much of God's world in a Korean city. Older and wearier Christians tend to see only the worst of the West creeping in and the worst of the East still hanging on, making so many of Asia's cities characterless hybrids of the worst of two worlds. But the boy under the umbrella was right. The city, with all its problems—its unemployment, its vice, its poverty, its greed, and disorder—is still God's world and the church cannot desert it. It is rapidly becoming the most pressing single challenge to the Christian faith in Korea.

Twenty years ago Seoul was a quiet, orderly town of about 250,000 people. Today its streets scream with the burden of a population of more than two million. All of Korea, it seems, is trying to live in Seoul, or at least in a city, for every year new thousands desert the village for the town. Most people still think of Korea as 70 or 75 per cent rural, but if preliminary reports of the 1960 census are correct, half of Korea's people are now living in cities, and the whole face of Korean society is changing. Curiously enough, the change is largely unconscious. Korea is a rural mind still unaware that its body has become urban.

Economically the shift to the city is even more sharply defined. The country's labor force comprises eleven million people, 60 per cent of whom are farmers, and only 12 per cent of whom are engaged in productive labor in factories or small plants. Yet the 12 per cent in the factories and plants now produce 60 per cent of the national income.

This is all the more remarkable when it is recalled that South Korea is traditionally the agricultural, not the industrial, half of the peninsula, and that its economy has suffered a succession of trip hammer blows that would have crushed a less tenacious people. First, the Japanese occupation stripped the peninsula of as much as could possibly be taken back to Japan. Next the Communists outmaneuvered the free world and seized all of North Korea, the rich, industrialized half of the country, and in so doing thought they had crippled South Korea for life. Finally, the Korea War with its waves of invasion reduced most of what was left in South Korea to rubble and ruin. "It is like a flower garden after a steam roller has rolled over it several times," commented one visitor. One-third of Korea's thirty million people, it is said, were either killed or made refugees in the war.

But the little republic of South Korea is fighting its way back economically as determinedly as it once turned back the Communist invaders. With massive aid from the United States, which reached a peak of $328,800,000 in 1957, declining to about $200,000,000 annually since then, South Korea's industrial production more than doubled in five short years after the war, and it is still rising. Electric power output (a key industrial factor) increased from 81,200 kw. in 1945 to 192,500 kw. in 1959. Thermo-electric power plants are utilizing South Korea's vast deposits of low-grade anthracite coal to replace the great waterpower reserves that were lost to the Communists in the north.

New factories are producing cement and fertilizer, glass and textiles, plastics and rayon, in a desperate effort to make the country economically self-supporting. But it is only a beginning. A recent government estimate puts Korea's imports at nineteen times her exports, while 70 per cent of the central government's revenues must be allocated to the nation's crushing defense burden—Korea has the fourth largest army in the world. No country can long survive with such an imbalanced economy. The result is inflation, unemployment, and depression.

Even for the employed, life is often unbearably drab. A factory worker's wages average less than thirty dollars a month. White-collar workers in the city do not average much more—fifty dollars a month for men, and twenty dollars for women. For many of these workers, life all too soon begins to lose its meaning. The city's deceptive veneer of sophisticated living, its surface gloss of soft pastel silks and neon lighted bars, its paved streets and automobiles, its black-market luxuries (now outlawed by the military government's austerity campaign) haunt them with the lure of a glittering way of life that is always just out of reach, leaving them forever unsatisfied. To some come the whispered temptations of the city's steaming underworld, the furtive promises of short cuts to luxury that only lead at last into the jungle of the slums, where packs of beggar boys fight like animals, where vice is king, and men and women cease almost to be human.

More to be pitied are the honest poor. One statistic is enough to pinpoint their plight. There were in Seoul, in the winter of 1961, 6,200 people who could find no shelter, who huddled together for warmth in caves or under bridges or in sewer culverts. In Korea's arctic winters, this meant death for all too many.

The first and immediate response of the Christian church to such need is charity and relief. This is not the complete answer of the church to the problem but where physical need is desperate and urgent, it must be the first answer.

In its 1960 report the Korea Association of Voluntary Agencies (mostly Protestant and Catholic mission-related agencies, but including some nonsectarian groups) stated that during the year its member agencies had brought into Korea more than 13 million dollars worth of relief supplies, ranging from food and clothing to heifers and medicines.

The major arm of the Protestant churches in this work of Christian compassion is Korea Church World Service. Convinced that Korea now has moved from a period of emergency relief into a period of chronic relief needs, Church World Service is successfully carrying out annual reductions in its direct relief program. But some idea of the scope of these activities is seen in the 1960 figures, when CWS brought in more than 50 million pounds of relief goods valued at $4,200,000. It served 154 feeding stations, giving 77,000 hungry people a daily hot meal of corn meal mush cooked with powdered milk. Local Korean church groups furnished the cooking facilities, the fuel, and the labor as their contribution to the feeding program. In addition to the feeding station program, several million pounds of flour, corn meal, corn syrup, canned meat, and cooking oil were given to needy families. Church World Service also distributed some 9 million pounds of relief supplies to groups of refugees building homes or reclaiming farmland in an effort to make themselves self-supporting again. And in the winter months, how many thousands of the destitute have been saved from freezing to death by gifts of CWS blankets and clothing, no one will ever know.

But the overwhelming physical needs are too great for any one agency to meet alone. The Oriental Missionary Society has distinguished itself with a unique ministry of relief to the neglected fisher folk of Korea's thousand islands. The activities of this agency were officially recognized by the Korean government, which recently decorated the Rev. Elmer Kilbourne for his organization of the society's work.

The Salvation Army's mobile soup kitchen runs by night through the most vicious slum areas in Seoul. It is a ride that can terrify the amateur social worker. Blackened, grotesque figures rise suddenly from the darkness under the bridges as the truck pulls to a stop, then as suddenly disappear when they are fed. Some return hesitantly to murmur thanks, remembering once again that they are human.

The work of Christian redemption is sometimes very slow, but ministering to society's outcasts is one way it can begin. It was to just such a one, a leper who returned to thank him, that Jesus said, "Thy faith hath made thee whole."

Among the neediest of all are Korea's orphans. But in an unparalleled way, Christians the world over have opened their hearts to take them in. No man has done more for them than a short, barrel chested farmer from Creswell, Oregon, Harry Holt. More than half of all the orphans rescued from Korean streets and placed in American homes owe their salvation to this one man.

A recent visitor to the Holt Orphanage outside Seoul, Mrs. Theodore Stevenson, writes, "It was alive with babies—babies in bassinets, babies crawling, crying, asleep on the floor; sick babies in isolation wards; and older children spilling over onto the playground. This was different from other Korean orphanages I had seen, for these were mixed-blood children, as the wavy or fair hair, the paler skin, and the round instead of slanting eyes, indicated. These were children abandoned by their Korean mothers and American fathers, and rejected by Korean society which can be very cruel to the different and unlike."

But Harry Holt, quoting Isaiah,—"Fear not: for I am with thee. I will bring thy seed from the East, and gather thee from the West . . ."—is fiercely determined that even the different shall find love. He is still looking for Western homes for his "seed from the East."

A much larger problem is the problem of the full blood Korean orphan. The war is long over, but there are still close to one hundred thousand of them, about sixty thousand in more than five hundred orphanages, and twenty-five thousand or more homeless children wandering the city streets and country roads. Less than half of these children are true orphans; the rest have simply been abandoned. In Pusan alone, Korea's second largest city, two thousand abandoned babies were picked up in 1960. But statistics cannot tell the story. "Not one of us will ever forget the living lifelessness of a starved baby in a Taegu clinic," reported Church World Service's Orphan Survey Team. "Here in one tiny, stunted body was compressed the reality of war, human blindness, and cruelty. That malnourished child represented uncounted mothers' heroic and defeated efforts to care for their own...."

Not all orphanages, unfortunately, are well run. Some alas, only exploit the orphan for private gain. The best ones are likely to be those managed by reputable Christian agencies like the Christian Children's Fund and World Vision, whose orphanages are of all denominational persuasions. The Christian Children's Fund in Korea has 92 orphanages serving some 12,500 children. A trained public health nurse gives supervision to the institutions. World Vision, whose energetic president, Dr. Bob Pierce, was the man who triggered Harry Holt's interest in Korean orphans, supports about thirteen thousand children in Korea. The World Vision Orphan Hospital, attached to the Presbyterian Hospital in Taegu, is the first hospital of its kind in Korea, and its Vocational Training High School, staffed by the Oriental Missionary Society, is helping two to three thousand orphans prepare for job competition in the wide world beyond the orphanage. (It was World Vision's Korean Orphan Choir that made such an overnight sensation on its recent tour of the United States.)

The Korean churches are just beginning to awaken to the possibilities and need of a new approach to the orphan problem. Some leaders are urging an adoption program for Korea that will take the orphans out of institutions and place them in Korean Christian homes for the individual love and care that is every child's deepest need. The largest private effort in this direction is the Foster Parents' Plan, which has placed 4,800 children in homes. Usually it is with a widow whose husband is dead, or lost in North Korea, or handicapped and unable to earn a living. The Foster Parents' Plan subsidizes such a home to enable it to feed and care for the extra child.

Miss Esther Laird, at the Methodist Community Center in Taejon, has been experimenting with a similar plan. Orphaned babies are kept in the nursery during the day, but at night thirty-two widows, who are employed in a sewing project, each take home a baby. What a difference a mother's love makes, even if it is only for the night. The babies lose their fear of strangers. They learn to talk earlier. And most striking of all, head beating, that bane of orphanage life that sets the children to thumping their heads rhythmically against the bed or wall or floor, completely disappears.

If any place in Korea can tug at the heartstrings more than an orphanage, it is a school for the blind. "Blind children," writes Mrs. Kelmore Spencer, superintendent of the Presbyterian Blind School in Chungju, "are still hidden in homes because of their parents' shame. They are still being sold or sent to sorcerers to learn the magic arts. To see those who have been taught nothing literally come to life after entering a home for the blind, where they are loved by their teachers and other blind children, continues to be an inexpressibly joyous experience. . . ."

The tragedy is that so much blindness in Korea is preventable. One frantic and ignorant mother poured gasoline into the eyes of her six-year-old son, thinking it would cure a painful and spreading infection, only to find that she had blinded him for life.

The care and education of these unfortunates has been one of the outstanding forms of Christian service in Korea ever since the pioneering days of Dr. Rosetta Hall and Dr. Alice Fish Moffett, who opened the first schools for the blind in Pyongyang. Today Christians are still the active core and center of the Advisory Committee for International Aid to the Blind in Korea, which co-ordinates service to schools enrolling some seven hundred blind children. Its chairman is Mrs. Mary Lee, a teacher in the Social Welfare Department of Ewha Women's University.

There is a blindness of the mind as well as of the eye. Korea's rate of illiteracy is only 22 per cent, which is low for Asia, thanks to the remarkable fifteenth century development of a Korean phonetic alphabet. Its ten vowels and fourteen consonants are infinitely easier to learn, of course, than the thousands of picture symbols that make up written Chinese, for example. And yet, until Christians rescued and revived the alphabet for use in the Korean Bible, it had fallen into disuse, scorned by Korean scholars as entirely too easy and fit only for women or slaves.

Curiously enough the highest rate of illiteracy in Korea is in the city of Seoul. To meet the challenge of this blindness of the mind, the Christian Literacy Society of Korea, representing seven major Korean denominations, has trained more than five thousand volunteer workers to teach literacy classes in churches and schools and has organized 2,225 reading clubs with a total membership of more than forty thousand. Each club is sent twenty of the Society's books. When all the members of the club have read a book and sent in brief reports on it, they are eligible to receive another book—up to a total of one hundred books. General Secretary Cynn-Young Ahn is concerned that the percentage of illiterates among Christians, though less than the national average, is not as much less as it was twenty years ago. "The Church has not been putting the same emphasis on being able to read one's Bible as in former years," Mr. Ahn says. To recapture this emphasis is his great hope. "Our aim is to make the Koreans a reading people, and to encourage Christians to read their Bibles with pleasure and from habit."

There is yet a broader and deeper response to human need to which the church in Korea is called. Its person to person ministry of mercy to the poor, the hungry, the naked, the fatherless, the illiterate, and the blind is only a first response to immediate need, the response of a compassionate heart. There must also be the response of the Christian conscience, a response that carries the church beyond charity to grapple with the roots of the social ills that make charity necessary. This, as Richard Niebuhr reminds us, means "taking the side of the poor, showing brotherhood and solidarity with those who are being threatened, placing one's self between them and the points of oppression. In this way a correction is brought into society and a sign is established of the world of peace, as it is meant and promised by God."

To look at You-Du Kang, you would not pick her as the type for the intense involvement that Christian responsibility sometimes seems to demand. She is just a slim, good-humored girl from a cultured family, with none of the serious and self-sacrificing look of the social martyr about her at all. But it was You-Du Kang who went to the military authorities after she was graduated from Ewha College, and said, "Send me out to the poorest, most backward mountain section of our country. With the men gone to war, the women must raise food for the nation. Let me go out to teach them how." So off she went, city-bred though she was, to take charge of a rural project under the supervision of the provincial government. You-Du won the confidence of the village women with her frankness and good spirits and they began to ask her, "Are you a Christian? We think you must be for we have heard that all Christians are honest."

Much later, as the tides of war swept back and forth across Korea, You-Du took to the road with thousands of fellow refugees and came at last to Pusan. Ever since, she has identified herself as fully and whole-heartedly with the hopes and fears of the overworked, underemployed, insecure people of that crowded city as she once unreservedly had given herself to the people of the mountains. She is the director of the Christian Community Center in Pusan, one of the six Methodist centers located in Korea's major cities. Unafraid, she has rescued many a waif from the pickpocket gangs that roam the streets of Pusan. She has so impressed some of the outcast gangs that she has been made an honorary member of the "Christian Beggars' Guild"! And so she goes steadily about her work, rescuing the fallen, getting to know the outcasts, slowly working them into a congenial fellowship, trying to interest them in school, in jobs, in anything that will lift them out of their old evil ways—and never failing to understand and love and bear gentle witness to the greater love of Jesus Christ.

Still another approach to the problems of the city is a new emphasis in the church on industrial evangelism. One young minister, a leader in the church's industrial evangelism program has had engineering training. "In January," he writes, "the chief engineer of the cement plant asked me to work in the plant as assistant designer in mechanics. My hope is that I myself can lead the laborers to God. I work in the plant eight hours a day; preach three to five times a week at the church. I am trying to organize the deacons and deaconesses

141

THE CHRISTIANS OF KOREA

to do the visiting in the homes and have two deacons preach each month. . . ." Students-in-Industry projects also have been tried successfully, notably in the cement manufacturing center of Sinki-ree.

No one pretends that the church in Korea has made more than a beginning of an approach to Christian involvement in the problems of society in the cities. Sometimes the younger generation is impatient for more concrete evidences of Christian concern and action as the processes of urbanization and industrialization accelerate in the new Korea. When 119 students and leaders from forty-one Korean colleges met in Inchon last year for a historic meeting of the Korean Student Christian Council (representing the Y.W.C.A., the Y.M.C.A., and the Korean Student Christian Movement) they joined in united study of a newly published booklet, *Church and Society.* There was a great eagerness to find Christian answers to the complex problems that were troubling them. It is interesting to note that, by way of bridging the way to a partial solution of one of Korea's most pressing international problems, the students had invited six Christian young people from Japan to share with them in the conference.

Where there is such concern and the beginnings of action, there is hope that Korea's multitude of city churches, as they point their steeples proudly to the sky, will not forget that their foundations rest, like any other building, in the common earth of the city. The chief cornerstone is Jesus Christ, who still prays not that the Father should take us out of the world but that He will keep us from evil.

7 | EDUCATION AND THE INNER CITADEL

W<small>HY DO YOU PASS UP THIS GOOD SCHOOL RIGHT</small> near your own home and walk so far to a school of the foreign religion?" a friend asked a Korean schoolboy who was going without breakfasts in order to get an education.

"I do it," he answered, "not only because they give me the best learning, but also the best religion."

The best learning and the best religion! Just such a life-giving balance of wisdom and faith was provided by the Christian mission almost from its inception.

Schools have been an integral part of the church's planning since 1884. At that time Dr. R. S. Maclay, superintendent of the Methodist Mission in Japan, accomplished the impossible task of persuading the isolationist, Christian persecuting Korean court to grant permission for the opening of a school and hospital in the Hermit Kingdom. The problem, however, always has been how to build Christian schools in which both parts of the combination—learning and religion —were kept vital and operative. In the early days and during the Japanese occupation, it was a struggle to keep the schools Christian. Lately, it has been equally difficult to keep the schools academically reputable.

When Appenzeller first opened his school in 1886, it was not the Christian faith that attracted students. They came for the foreign learning, and even this was not much of an attraction. Students had to be paid to attend Pai Chai Academy (Hall for Rearing Useful Men). For a while the missionaries did not even dare hold prayers for the students, so fearful were they of anti-Christian government reaction. The students were equally fearful. "I gave a student a tract on faith to copy," wrote Mr. Appenzeller, "He took it to his room, read it a little . . . [and] came back with it saying, 'If it were known that I was at work on a tract like this, my head would be taken off. . . .' "

Afraid or not, students attending the Christian schools learned quickly about the new religion. The most popular classes were those teaching English, and for a textbook the missionaries used the Bible, not always, however, with the desired linguistic results. One student, trying out his English, described a conversation with a friend by writing, "I opened my mouth and I said unto him. . . ."

But make no mistake. Tentative, uncertain, and slightly ridiculous though these first Christian experiments in education in Korea may seem today, they were the serious beginnings of an educational revolution that was to shatter the grip of the dead past and open Korea's mind to the future.

Traditionally, education in Korea was rote memorization of the Chinese classics. Upon mastery of the classics depended a man's hope not only for academic recognition but for political advancement as well, for the Yi dynasty's political appointments were made largely on the basis of the annual literary examinations. It was universally assumed that the classics taught all that was necessary for the proper regulation of society.

The highest ambition of the graduates of the old Korean schools was to compete successfully in the great national examinations in Seoul. Every year, out of the hundreds who might enter the "Great Examination," only thirty-three could expect to pass; but success meant achieving the pinnacle of literary fame and immediate appointment by the king to an official position. No matter how humble his beginnings, a successful candidate's future was secure and his social status unshakeable.

The flaw in the system, of course, was that the ability to weave a few thousand Chinese characters into poems or commentaries on obscure philosophic passages is no test of a man's character and fitness to rule. Worse yet, by the nineteenth century corruption had so abused the examination procedures that 90 per cent of the winners, it is said, owed their victory more to favoritism and bribery than to scholarship. A fatal defect in Confucian ethics was its exaltation of personal loyalties above principle. The acceptance of bribes was easily rationalized as fulfillment of the duty to provide for one's family and relatives—a higher virtue than adherence to mere abstract principles like honesty or justice.

Korea, as it neared the twentieth century, needed both integrity and learning. It needed "a true education of heart and mind," but this the ancient classical platitudes, however noble they sounded on paper, could not provide. Indeed, the new Korea demanded new ideas, new methods, new schools, and new men, and these she found at first only in the Christian schools. By the beginning of the twentieth century Christian schools were easily the most popular and crowded schools in the country. Where else could one learn mathematics and science and all the tantalizingly new learning of the modern world? Where else could girls go to school? Hundreds of primary schools were established. No church considered itself complete without a day school attached.

"We are in the midst of an educational revolution," wrote missionaries in Syenchun in 1908. "Schools spring up in a night. . . . The old Confucian scholars lose their proud seats, giving place to those who know both Chinese and Western learning. So strong has been the leadership of the church that . . . the course of study used in Christian schools has been the pattern for unbelievers' schools as well. During the year probably as many as five or six hundred primary and night schools, claiming to teach Western [learning] have been started by officials and other unbelievers in our territory. The church schools are in the lead of all and influence all."

Christian high schools also sprang up from Syenchun in the north to Mokpo in the far south. At Kaesong the famous Anglo-Korean school of Tchi-Ho Yoon began experimenting with the radical theory that students should learn to work. Classical scholars were aghast. "Workers work; scholars teach or rule or write; they do not work." When Christians questioned these Confucian precepts, they started another revolution in education.

Baron Yoon's first school report put it very clearly to the Methodist Church: "We must remember that industrial training is more useful to a Korean today than mere literary education." His school's policy—"the first conscious effort made in a mission school to give industrial education to Korean youth as an end in itself"—was most practical. The school taught the boys skills they could practice with the least outlay of money and time after graduation, using materials and tools such as could be obtained in Korea or neighboring countries.

Nowhere was the revolution wrought by the Christian schools more radical than in the field of education for women. Confucianism stripped a woman of all will but her husband's, no provision was made for her education. What a change three generations of Christians have made! Today Korea has, in Ewha Women's University, the largest women's college in the world—a union venture supported by American Methodists and the United Church of Canada.

In 1910 Ewha Girls' School, which was the first school for girls in all Korea, shocked the old-fashioned by introducing college grade work for women. Under its college principal, Miss Lulu Frey, there began a transforming ferment in Korean society that revolutionized everything from women's clothes to public health. Women's role in Korean society has never since been quite the same.

The first Christian college, however,—in fact, the first college of any kind in the modern sense—was a co-operative venture of Presbyterians and Methodists, Union Christian College (Soongsil University), which was founded by Dr. W. M. Baird in Pyongyang in 1906. Its emphasis on a concentrated Christian education for the children of believers rather than on education for all in competition with government schools has given the Korean church more college-trained ministers than any other school in Korea.

In 1915, using rooms rented from the Korean Y.M.C.A. in Seoul, Chosen Christian College (now Yonsei University) was organized. This was also a union venture and Dr. H. G. Underwood acted as president until his untimely death the next year. He was succeeded by the founder of Severance Hospital, Dr. O. R. Avison. As one of Korea's most prestigious universities, Yonsei has probably poured more Christians into the political and cultural life of the nation than any other one institution.

Since the Korea War a number of smaller Christian colleges have opened their doors. Refugees from North Korea, sturdily self-reliant and loyal to their own traditions, reactivated Union Christian College, which had been closed by the Japanese and destroyed by the Communists. Dr. Sung-Nak Kim, formerly of the Korean Presbyterian Church in Los Angeles, is president, succeeding Dr. Kyung-Chik Han. The new campus is on gentle hills across the Han River.

In the southeast eight Korean presbyteries, long eager for a college they could call their own, chose Dr. Archibald Campbell to found Keimyung Christian College in Taegu in 1954. Just last year the college elected its first Korean president, Dr. Tae-Sik Synn. Located on a hill commanding a magnificent view of the city, the college now has an enrollment of five hundred and serves an area with a population of more than 5 million people.

Southern Presbyterians meanwhile established the first Christian college in the southwestern provinces when Taejon College opened its doors to its first students. Its president is a second generation Korea missionary, Dr. John Talmadge.

The latest experiment in Christian higher education is Seoul Women's College, founded by the Presbyterian Church in Korea in 1961 as a residential college, training girls for rural community development. One of Korea's outstanding sociologists is its president, Dr. Evelyn Koh. She is a woman who is equally at home at embassy teas or at anti-concubinage rallies, and is as effective speaking quietly and earnestly to a girl about the claims of Jesus Christ as she is designing a new and radically improved latrine for the Korean village.

Something of the enthusiastic intensity and sacrificial spirit with which Korean Christians support their colleges is shown in a story that Mrs. Sun Ae Chou tells about how her church's smallest and poorest district on Cheju Island raised money for one room in the new dormitory at Seoul Women's College.

"How can we raise six hundred dollars?" the Cheju Island women asked themselves. "That is the cost of one room. But it is too much."

"Perhaps we could go up into the mountains and gather *kosari* (a choice and expensive wild herb used in cooking)," suggested one of the women. "We could take it to Seoul when we go to the national meeting. If we sell it there, we will make quite a bit of money. *Kosari* is expensive in the city."

Estimating that it would take two years to complete the project, for six hundred dollars was a large sum of money for so poor a group to try to raise, the women set to work at once.

It was a great day for the women of little Cheju Island

when they stood up proudly as equals with the well-dressed women from larger and richer districts and reported to the national meeting that they, too, had brought six hundred dollars for a room in the new dormitory.

"How did you do it?" the others asked.

The leader of the Cheju Island group smiled and held up a bundle of kosari in her hand. "We can do everything in Christ our Lord, who strengthens us," she said.

At the other end of the educational scale from the Christian colleges are the Bible Clubs. About thirty years ago Dr. Francis Kinsler, a missionary in Pyongyang, became concerned about the plight of the thousands of neglected, underprivileged children of the slums who could not afford the fees required in the public schools and who were drifting into undisciplined street gangs. Enlisting the help of Christian college and seminary students, Dr. Kinsler began to gather the unschooled waifs into Bible Clubs that were, in effect, short-term day schools. The Bible Clubs teach Bible, history, language, arithmetic, first aid, geography, and physical education. Seventy thousand children and more are enrolled in Bible Clubs all over the country, and the character transformation wrought in these poorest of the poor, these children of the depressed and defeated, is a miracle. Just to watch a ten-year-old girl from a one-room shack stand up, poised and assured, to lead a rally of six thousand Bible Clubbers in prayer and Bible reading and hymn singing is to see Christian leadership created out of the most unlikely material in the whole country.

The Korean church has developed three types of educational programs for training its professional leadership: Bible institutes for the preparation of unordained lay leaders for the rural church; night seminaries for preliminary training toward either ordained or unordained Christian service, usually of students with substandard academic preparation; and the major theological seminaries.

A Rockefeller Foundation world survey of theological seminaries made in 1957 revealed the startling fact that there were more students studying for the Protestant ministry in Korea than in any other country in Asia, Africa, or Latin America. In fact the enrollment in just one Korean seminary, the Presbyterian Theological Seminary in Seoul, almost equaled the number of ministerial students in all the Protestant seminaries of the great subcontinent of India.

Since the day in 1901 when the Rev. Samuel A. Moffett gathered two converts in a room in his home and began the first systematic theological training for a Christian ministry in Korea, the Seoul seminary has graduated 1,974 students. In recent years church schisms have sharply reduced the number of students, but, interestingly enough, it probably numbers more converted Communists among its graduates than any other seminary in the world. Fifty-five North Korean soldiers, captured in the war and converted in prisoner-of-war camps, have taken its theological course and are now serving the church.

An encouraging factor connected with the rise of enrollments in the seminaries is the generally high quality of the students. There is also a new and promising generation of theologians on the seminary faculties. Scholars like Dr. Harold Hong of the Methodist Seminary, the Rev. Tong-Hwan Moon at the Hankuk Seminary (R.O.K. Presbyterian),

Dr. Tae-Dong Han, at Yonsei University's Department of Theology, Dr. Yun-Kuk Kim at the Presbyterian Theological Seminary, and the Rev. Sang-Chung Pak, who has been called from the Seoul Seminary of the Holiness Church to head the National Christian Council's Department of Youth Work, contribute regularly to the monthly magazine *Christian Thought*, which has caught the attention of Korea's non-Christian intellectuals in a new way.

Another new venture in theological education is the Anglican experiment in Christian community at St. Michael's Seminary near Seoul. Faculty and students are brought together in total participation in a program emphasizing the unity of worship, study, and service.

Today the Christian schools in Korea are facing a whole new set of problems. Korea has 3,800,000 elementary school students, eight hundred thousand junior and senior high school students, and about one hundred thousand college students enrolled in some sixty-five colleges. Once more than half of the students in Korea were studying in Christian schools, now only a small fraction are registered. Of Korea's one hundred thousand college students, for example, only about fourteen thousand attend Christian colleges. Government supported education has outstripped the Christian educational system not only in numbers of students but also to a certain extent in scholastic standing.

Two of the major problems facing all colleges, governmental as well as Christian, are over-enrollment and underemployment. As high as three out of four college graduates are unable to find work after graduation. As a consequence the military government is looking with a jaundiced eye on Korea's swollen college enrollments. New educational regulations will undoubtedly considerably reduce the number of college students allowed to matriculate. How can underdeveloped Korea, the government asks with considerable justification, afford to have the same percentage of college students in relation to the total population as highly industrialized Britain? But all this, of course, only adds to the pent up frustrations of Korea's students—restless, excitable, impatient for quick results, and bitterly disappointed that their April, 1960, revolution has not yet given them the new and perfect Korea of which they dream.

Christian leaders, too, are reviewing their educational policies. How large a network of Christian schools can the church in Korea afford to maintain? Even with generous help from American and Canadian churches, few schools can compete on an equal basis in equipment and maintenance with the government system. And yet, so unique is the contribution of the Christian school, and so distasteful the alternative of monolithic government education (without the stimulating and liberalizing influence of the private school), that no Christian in Korea seriously advocates the abandonment of the Christian schools.

In the Christian school there is a flexibility and freedom for pioneering in new techniques, an emphasis on ethics as well as intellect, and above all, a redeeming faith that alone is adequate to nourish what Dr. George Paik has called the "inner citadel." "Our cities, homes, and factories can and must be rebuilt," says Dr. Paik, former minister of education and until recently president of Yonsei University. ". . . [but] what we must safeguard above all is the Inner Citadel . . . the integrity of the people. It is their minds and their morals, their intelligence, their sense of duty, their spiritual resilience. . . ."

Christians and non-Christians alike have traditionally looked to the Christian school in Korea for the maintenance of the inner citadel. "Christians," said the well-known non-Christian president of Korea University, a secular private school, "are the conscience of Korea." There is no easy road to faith and integrity, even in a Christian school, and discouragements come often. But even in the midst of frustrations, one offsetting incident, one spark of spiritual integrity can make everything seem worthwhile again to those who work with the church in education.

A graduate of a little Christian high school went to Seoul. There he found a job in an army store where the fiery pressures of the city's black market operations come to a white-hot peak. Not long after the boy had begun work, he came home one night with his face badly cut and bruised. "What happened?" he was asked.

"I wouldn't do what some of the others wanted me to do," he said, "so I was beaten up on the way home."

"What did they want you to do?"

"They were trying to get me to cheat the store, but I couldn't do it. They knew that I was a Christian, and I knew that God was depending on me," he said.

When a Christian school produces this kind of integrity in a land whose future may well depend on the rediscovery of public and private integrity, then indeed the long hours of the Christian educator are not wasted.

8 | MEDICINE AND MIRACLES

MEDICINE IS OUR SUBSTITUTE FOR MIRACLES," A missionary to China once said, not to disparage miracles but in tribute to his medical colleagues. In Korea, too, Christian medicine has worked its miracles.

During the Korea War an officer of the United States Army dropped into a Christian hospital for a visit. A triple amputee was demonstrating how he could walk with one artifical leg and one peg leg, manipulating a crutch with the hook that replaced his missing hand. Suddenly he wheeled around and said to the officer, "I was nothing but a thing crawling on the ground. Now I am a man again. . . ."

It is no small miracle to take a thing and help to make him man again, to give hope to those who have lost all hope, but such is the work of Christian medicine in Korea. It ministers both to the body and to the soul. When it makes a man, it seeks to make him a whole man, new and alive in Jesus Christ, renewed—not just patched up.

The first accomplished miracle of the Christian physician

in Korea was the opening of that closed land to the gospel less than twenty years after the bloodiest massacre of Christians the country had ever seen. When Dr. Horace Allen's skilled hands saved the life of the Queen's nephew in 1884, the anti-foreign stone tablets erected by the Tai Won Kun bearing the decree that had touched off the persecutions of 1866 were still standing:

"The barbarians from beyond the seas have violated our borders and invaded our land. If we do not fight we must make a treaty with them. Those who favor making a treaty sell their country. Let this be a warning to ten thousand generations."

It was Allen's miracle of healing that first began to remove the aura of menace that clouded the image of the foreigner in the Korean mind. His reward was permission to open a royal hospital under mission auspices, the first of the Christian hospitals of Korea. Other able medical missionaries followed in Allen's footsteps and further won the gratitude of the populace by stemming the tides of death in the great cholera epidemics of 1886 and 1895. Canadian O. R. Avison was appointed personal physician to the king and Dr. Lillias Horton (Mrs. H. G. Underwood) attended the queen. Up to that time the queen had been treated by Korean doctors who, because they were men, were forbidden to touch the person of the queen. "They felt her pulse by using a cord, one end of which was fastened about her wrist and the other, carried into the next room, was held in the doctor's fingers," wrote Mrs. Underwood. "The royal tongue . . . was protruded through a slit in a screen for the physician's observation."

The breaking of these ancient taboos by the introduction

of modern medical science was the second miracle of Christian medicine in Korea.

Christian physicians and nurses founded the first adequate hospitals and dispensaries in Korea. They established the first nurses' training schools, the first leprosarium, the first tuberculosis sanitorium. Medical missionaries were the first to check the ravages of epidemics such as Asiatic cholera, bubonic plague, and smallpox. They pioneered in public health and sanitation—in fact, there was no word in the Korean language for sanitation until Christians introduced the concept.

No country in Asia, it has been said, paid more attention to medicine than old Korea. To Korea came Japan for medical knowledge. To Korea came China for drugs, some of them like ginseng, worth their weight in gold in ancient times. Surgery was unknown, but acupuncture, cautery, and treatment with herbs were well-developed medical sciences. And yet, while there was considerable skill and wisdom among the best practitioners, the whole field of medicine was debased by shamanist superstitions and local ignorance. Basic medical textbooks, derived from the Chinese, had not been revised for three hundred years.

Some of the old practices still linger, being spread more widely than many realize. Most rural villages still have a shamanist sorcerer or witch ministering to the weak and credulous, though outdated and overdiluted penicillin may now be substituted for the once valued powdered tiger skull. But at least the go-betweens no longer complicate the problems of medical practice. Early missionary dentists complained that a number of poor unfortunates had perfectly good teeth pulled because they seated themselves in the doctor's chair and indicated the location of the aching tooth. Only too late the dentist would discover that the real owner of the aching tooth was thirty miles away and that the man in the chair was only the go-between representing the patient in the ancient fashion.

The coming of the Christian hospital was like a fresh wind blowing away ancient superstitions and musty practices, relieving fear and suffering in amazing ways, and bringing the best of healing even to the poorest of the poor.

The principal diseases in those early days were the chills and fevers that were called the ague, and smallpox—Koreans did not even count their children until after they had had smallpox. Typhus fever and Asiatic cholera swept through the land in great epidemics, and finally there was tuberculosis, which was everywhere.

Both Dr. Allen of the Presbyterian mission and Dr. W. B. Scranton of the Methodist mission trained hospital assistants and drug clerks. Out of these early beginnings, and on the foundations of the old royal hospital, Dr. Avison started what is now Severance Hospital and the Medical School of Yonsei University. This was the first and finest modern medical center in the entire country, combining the joint efforts of Presbyterians, Methodists, Anglicans, and United Church of Canada. The first seven graduates, the first doctors in the modern sense to be educated in Korea, received their diplomas in 1908. Even as late as 1954 the Korean government reported that more than a third of all Korea's licensed physicians were Severance graduates.

The seven Severance graduates were not the country's first Korean doctors, however. Often forgotten is the fact that the first Korean physician to practice Western medicine was not a man, but a woman. In 1887 Dr. Meta Howard, of the Woman's Division of the Methodist Board of Missions, began medical work in Korea "by women for women," inaugurating a form of service that led to the establishment of the first Women's Hospital, now a part of Ewha Women's University in Seoul. Dr. Rosetta Hall, taking up the same work, trained and sent to America Mrs. Esther Kim Pak, who was graduated from Johns Hopkins University. She returned to Korea in 1900 as the country's first Korean doctor of modern medicine, serving her country faithfully until her death in 1911. To appreciate the radical revolution, the miracle, that this represented, it must be remembered that in 1900 Korean girls were scarcely considered worth medical treatment, much less medical training.

With infinite patience and loving care Christian medicine fought its pioneering fight for adequate medical care for all. By the time of the Japanese conquest, so firmly were the Christian hospitals established in the affections and confidence of the Korean people that not even the new government's vigorous sponsorship of its own hospitals and health services could displace the Christian institutions in prestige and in the hearts of the people.

By 1930 there were forty-three government and public hospitals in Korea and forty-one private, non-Christian hospitals, as compared to only thirty Christian centers for medical work, most of them small and inadequate. But still the people, when they could, came to the Christian hospitals. "Why?" asked a Korean doctor. And an old Korean grandmother replied, "Because only Christians are kind to strangers."

This is the third miracle of Christian medicine in Korea—the miracle that the Christian faith works in the practice of medicine itself. As one of the leading Christian Korean doctors said after the war, "We must teach the medical students the difference between a business and a profession. They must learn that a hospital is a place to help people, not to make money."

It is this note of personal compassion in Christian medicine that turns it to the care of the hopeless and the helpless, that calls it to minister to those whom society too often has passed by—the cough-wracked victim of tuberculosis, the sufferer from leprosy, the amputee.

Tuberculosis is the number one health menace in Korea today. Every ten minutes a Korean dies of TB. Three out of every four persons are infected; one out of every thirty has a potentially dangerous case. America has eight times as many people as Korea, but only four hundred thousand active cases to Korea's eight hundred thousand. And in America there are 125,000 beds for the care of the tubercular, while Korea has only ten thousand hospital beds for all diseases.

In 1928 Dr. Sherwood Hall opened a Methodist sanitorium in Haiju, the first in all Korea. The great united thrust against tuberculosis, however, came only in 1954, when Presbyterians, Methodists, Seventh-day Adventists, Mennonites, United Lutherans, Disciples of Christ, and the United Church of Canada acted together to check the ravages of the disease. Through Church World Service they organized a nationwide network of sixteen chest clinics, which co-operated with the Christian hospitals of the various denominations. Under the leadership of Dr. Ernest B. Struthers of the Canadian mission, and more recently of Dr. Kenneth Scott, the clinics now treat a third of all the ambulatory tuberculosis patients receiving treatment in Korea.

The Southern Presbyterian Graham Memorial Tuberculosis Hospital, for example, treats over a thousand patients a month, and turns up at least five new cases every day.

At Severance Hospital, which has the first and largest clinic, Dr. Struthers pioneered in proving that tuberculosis can be effectively treated even on an out-patient basis and at very small cost. He inaugurated the first home visiting program in Korea, and succeeded in X-raying—for the first time in the whole Far East, probably—a large proportion (87.5 per cent) of the families of TB patients. Exposed as they are to the infection, they are the most common carriers of it.

The problems of proper treatment in Korea are incredibly difficult, however. A typical example is the case of Yung-Chai Chun, eighteen years old, who is trying to support a handicapped father, a younger brother and a younger sister, and cure himself of tuberculosis at the same time. According to the doctor's orders he must have rest and receive treatment, but how can he rest when he must feed his family? He hasn't the strength for much but shining shoes. By working diligently he earns five dollars a month, with which he sends his little brother to primary school. His fifteen-year-old sister helps him earn a living by peddling briquettes of coal from house to house, but she rarely gets more than the equivalent of four or five days' work a month. Fortunately Church World Service soup kitchens provide the family with soup morning and night, and Christian social workers are also helping the family.

The chances are that Yung-Chai's life will be saved, for 88 per cent of those with early infections and 60 per cent of those with advanced cases who come to the chest clinics for treatment become noninfectious in six months. This is largely due to new medical techniques, but it is an astounding record for the Far East, nonetheless.

As with tuberculosis, so with the treatment of leprosy— the pioneers were Christians. The oldest leprosarium in the country is the Southern Presbyterian center near Suchon, the fifty-three-year-old R. M. Wilson Leprosy Colony, which is named in honor of its founder. Assisted by American Leprosy Missions, Inc., the Colony cares for 1,140 patients. Patient helps patient in this Christian center, where the church has a membership of more than eight hundred. The blind and the hopelessly crippled are ministered to by the strong and fit, who help by raising vegetables and chickens and pigs.

The Colony even has a Bible school, surely the only Leper Theological Institute in Asia. Amazingly enough, twenty-two of the school's thirty students come from other leprosaria attracted by this unique opportunity for training for Christian service.

Since treatment techniques now give some hope of cure, and the number of arrested cases is increasing, the problem of discharging patients into unfriendly communities faces Christian medical workers more sharply than ever, according to Dr. Stan Topple. Patients hesitate to go back home when social pressures may drive them away again and when tragedy so often dogs their lives.

In the case of amputees, too, only the Christians seem to care. Dr. Reuben Archer Torrey, Jr., who lost his own right arm on the Burma Road during World War II after years of service as a missionary in China, discovered in Korea how God could use his misfortune to help others. When the call came, "Help us do something about the thirty thousand amputee war casualties," the fifty-eight year old Torrey responded and began life all over again. He proved time after time to even the most handicapped that a man need not accept helplessness simply because he has lost a limb. Working out of the Church World Service Amputee Rehabilitation Center in Taejon, which he had helped to found, Dr. Torrey taught Korean amputees how, with artificial limbs, they could face up to life with dignity and self-respect.

It is hard for an amputee to feel too sorry for himself as he watches the energetic new director of the rehabilitation center, Mr. John Steensma, hard at work on plans for relocating the center to Seoul where greater emphasis can be placed on job placement of vocationally trained amputees. Mr. Steensma, who comes from the Christian Reformed Church, has lost both his hands.

In eight years of operation, up through 1960, the Taejon Center and its co-operating units in Severance Hospital, Taegu Presbyterian Hospital, and the Presbyterian Medical Center at Chonju, have served 3,574 amputees.

The Korea War dealt a cruel blow to medical work. At the some moment that it increased emergency demands on the country's slender medical resources, it virtually wiped out the hospitals that were equipped to deal with such taxing conditions. Of the fifty-four hospitals in Korea at that time, all but six were rendered inoperative by the explosive waves of invasion from the north.

One result of the terrifying destruction has been a strategic change in the church's over-all medical policy. Not all the hospitals have been rebuilt. Instead churches and missions are concentrating on establishing a limited number of fully-staffed, fully-equipped, top-grade medical centers. In turn, these medical centers are expected to "assist professionally . . . promote and supervise outlying medical clinics and whatever other satellite medical units may be established," as one denominational report puts it.

A measure of the continuing effectiveness of the Christian medical program is the virulence of Communist propaganda attacks upon it. Communist Radio Pyongyang recently devoted a full fifteen minutes to a hate-filled tirade against two medical missionaries, Dr. and Mrs. Kenneth Scott. These two blood-thirsty American missionaries, said the Communists, were daily draining the blood from two hundred helpless orphans, selling it at great profit to the top American general at Eighth U.S. Army headquarters in Seoul.

Dr. Scott, a surgeon, is one of 144 doctors (including 72 residents and 25 interns) at Severance, the largest of Korea's Christian medical centers. Severance includes the 250-bed hospital and Yonsei Medical College in which Dr. Scott is a professor. A new Severance Medical Center on the Yonsei campus is being built around a half-million dollar Memorial Chest Clinic donated by the Eighth U.S. Army in memory of the thirty thousand American soldiers who died in defense of Korea's freedom.

But just to set the record straight, let it be stated that Dr. Scott sells no blood to the U.S. Army. He gives it away free to the poor. Between January and October, 1961, Severance used 560 precious bottles of blood for transfusions for non-paying patients. The cost to the hospital, three thousand dollars; the cost to the patients, nothing. Dr. Scott's specialty is chest surgery. Last year he operated free of charge on thirty-eight patients, and the hospital had to turn away four times as many more cases because of lack of funds.

Mrs. Scott is director of the Crippled Children's Center at Yonsei where hundreds of children receive post-polio treatment. Last year pretty Penny Defore, daughter of movie and TV star Don Defore, worked at the Center, helping the youngsters put on their braces and then showing them how to walk. The eighteen-year-old had come all the way from Hollywood with a "crazy urge" to help Korean orphans, and she put in five hard days a week caring for the little ones.

Two primary problems associated with medical practice in Korea are the dearth of trained physicians and nurses, and the concentration of medical personnel in the cities, particularly in the capital. Statistically, Korea has only three and one-third doctors per ten thousand people, and only one and one-half nurses per ten thousand. More than a half of her larger towns have no resident doctor.

The larger Christian medical centers are necessarily located in the cities, but their geographical distribution is extensive. By an ingenious combination of satellite clinics and mobile teams for village visitation, they are reaching the medically isolated in an unmatched way. In the eastern province of Kangwondo, for example, the newest and one of the most modern hospitals in Korea has been opened jointly by Methodists and the United Church of Canada. The Wonju Union Christian Hospital is the only general hospital in an area of two hundred thousand people, and its establishment was greeted by a Canadian staff member, Dr. Florence Murray, as "the biggest event of 1959."

Methodists also have built the only Christian hospital in Inchon, the busy port west of Seoul. The Seventh-day Adventists, world-famed for their medical work, have an excellent medical center on the eastern outskirts of Seoul and a smaller unit in Pusan.

The Southern Presbyterian Medical Center in Chunju made news a few years ago when the wife of the American Ambassador chose it for an elective operation, startling the country with this demonstration of her faith that top-flight medical care was not limited to the capital city. Southern Presbyterians also operate the Kwangju Tuberculosis Hospital and the Leprosy Colony in Soonchun and have the distinction of maintaining the largest number of medical missionaries in the country.

In Pusan, Australian Presbyterians support one of the best-loved institutions in the southeast, the Il Sin Women's Hospital. Although the hospital has only seventy-five beds, the average midnight bed-count is eighty-five, and reaches as high as 114. "But there is a limit to the number of army cots available to fit into corridors," says Dr. Helen Mackenzie, the superintendent. "Those due for discharge often spend the morning sitting on someone else's bed because their beds are needed for the early morning rush of patients who come into labour during the night." Dr. Mackenzie and her sister Catherine Mackenzie, a nurse, received high recognition from Queen Elizabeth II in her 1962 New Year Honors list, which named them Members of the British Empire (M.B.E.).

The Salvation Army in Yong Dong, the Southern Baptists in Pusan, and the Friends in Kunsan all operate hospitals that carry an unusually high proportion of non-paying patients. The percentage at the Wallace Memorial Baptist Hospital in Pusan, for example, runs as high as 60 per cent.

Increasingly important in over-all medical policy is rural medical outreach through clinics such as those operated by the United Church of Canada in Iri, and by the United Presbyterians in Andong and Pohang. The latter two are supervised and assisted by the Presbyterian Hospital in Taegu, whose remarkably efficient staff of fifty-three Korean doctors has won high praise from government observers. The whole hospital is organized in a unique way for rural, medical evangelism. Emphasis is on all three words: rural, because the countryside is unreached; medical, because of the overwhelming physical needs; and evangelism, because the greatest miracle of all in Christian medical work is the cure of souls added to the cure of bodies.

"At the center of all our hospital work and program," writes Dr. Howard Moffett, the superintendent of the Taegu institution, "is our evangelistic effort." The staff is voluntarily organized into a "preaching society," in which all participate. A typical medical-evangelistic mobile clinic trip included four doctors, two nurses, one pharmacist, one hospital chaplain, and a driver-mechanic. The group took a week's exhausting trek through three provinces, treating patients in the villages, holding roadside demonstrations on health problems, giving medical lectures, making health surveys, and holding evangelistic services every night. They worked from daybreak prayer meeting time until midnight. More than

1,200 patients were given free treatments, and hundreds asked to know more about the Lord Jesus Christ of whom the doctors and nurses spoke so freely.

Testimonies from former patients are not uncommon in Korea's Christian hospitals. The medical center in Chonju, for instance, reports some six hundred to seven hundred conversions every year. At Taegu former patients, reinforced by the witness of the rural clinics, have started more than one hundred new churches where no churches were before.

Dr. Howard Moffett has written about a young man who was brought into the hospital after a street brawl. "Bruised and battered, with a broken jaw and a number of missing teeth, he was not very co-operative. Our chief of dentistry, Dr. Pyun, a highly skilled oral surgeon just returned from speciality work at the University of Pennsylvania, was hard put to it to get him quieted down and patched up. Dr. Pyun is also a deeply spiritual man, and as the days passed he quietly spoke to the young man about his need for more than physical repair. . . .

"About ten days later Dr. Pyun brought into my office a letter from the patient, who had been discharged. He wrote that because of the expert and amazingly kindly care he had received, he had made a further study of the Christian religion . . . he now wanted us to know that he had made the decision to follow Christ. . . ."

* * *

These are the Christians of Korea—the doctors, the nurses, the patients, and even the visitors in the hospitals. Count among them both the orphan in the Children's Hospital, his tiny wrist less than half as thick as a man's thumb, and the doctor who saved his life. Remember the seventeen-year-old spastic who was so grateful for treatment that he tried to pay for it with his own blood. The Christians are of all kinds and all classes. Some cannot even read their own Bibles yet, and others have Ph.D.'s from Yale. They include beggar boys and the President of the Republic, farmers and factory workers, college professors and janitors.

Some of them are very rich, like the textile industrialist who donated a new brick dormitory to a Christian college. Some have enough for a comfortable living, but give even that to God. One country elder contributed his life savings, two hundred dollars, to build a new church in his village and then, wanting to contribute even more, came into the hospital to ask if he could sell one of his eyes as a donation to the building fund. He wept when a Christian doctor gently talked him out of his determination to sacrifice the eye for the church.

Others have almost nothing, like the young refugee mother who lost her right arm at the shoulder and her right leg while trying to save her little boy from an onrushing train. During her hospitalization in Taegu, five women in her ward accepted Christ, testifying that the reason for their decision was the radiant triumph of this Christian woman in the face of her great personal tragedy. She now lives in a four by five foot room in a back alley and earns only twenty-five cents a day but tithes faithfully and cheerfully.

"We have been much humbled," a missionary says, "by knowing such people. . . . They are among the 'first in the Kingdom of Heaven!'" They are the Christians of Korea.

BIBLIOGRAPHY

SPACE forbids footnote citations in the text. Let me, at least, acknowledge in the list of works below my deep indebtedness to others whose writings on Korea have been consulted with pleasure and profit.—s.h.m.

The Horace N. Allen Papers. (MSS in the New York Public Library, Manuscript Room), [1884-1910].

Allen, Roland. "The Nevius Method in Korea," *World Dominion*, July, 1931.

The Anglican Church in Korea. Seoul, Korea: [1959].

Annual Report, 1888. New York: Board of Foreign Missions, Presbyterian Church in the U.S.A., 1889.

Beere, L. O. and Rees, W. E. *Corea*. London: Society for the Propagation of the Gospel, 1935.

Blair, William N. *The Korea Pentecost and Other Experiences on the Missionary Field*. New York: Board of Foreign Missions of the Presbyterian Church in the U.S.A., 1908.

Brown, Arthur Judson. *The Korean Conspiracy Case*. Northfield, Mass.: The Northfield Press, 1912.

Brown, Arthur Judson. *Report of a Second Visit to China, Japan and Korea*. New York: Board of Foreign Missions of the Presbyterian Church in the U.S.A., 1909.

Brown, G. T. "Missions and Unity, A Study of the Relationship between the Missionary Enterprise and the Ecumenical Movement." Unpublished Ph.D. dissertation, Union Theological Seminary, Richmond, Va., 1958.

Chun, S. C. "Schism and Unity in the Protestant Churches of Korea." Unpublished Ph.D. dissertation, Yale University. New Haven, Conn., 1955.

Clark, Allen D. History of the Korean Church. Seoul, Korea: Christian Literature Society of Korea, [1961].

Clark, Allen D., ed. Prayer Calendar of Christian Missions in Korea and General Directory, 1961. Seoul, Korea: Christian Literature Society of Korea, 1961.

Clark, C. A. The Nevius Plan for Mission Work in Korea. Seoul, Korea: Y.M.C.A. Press, 1937.

Corfe, C. J. The Anglican Church in Corea. London: Rivington & Co., 1906.

Dallet, Charles. Histoire de l'Eglise de Corée. Paris, France: Victor Palmé, 1874. 2 vols.

Fenwick, M. C. The Church of Christ in Corea. New York: Geo. H. Doran Co., 1911.

Fifty Years of Light. Seoul, Korea: Women's Foreign Missionary Society of the Methodist Episcopal Church, 1938.

Grad (Grajdanzev), Andrew Jonah. Modern Korea. New York: John Day Co., 1944.

Gale, J. S. Korea in Transition. New York: Board of Foreign Missions, Presbyterian Church in the U.S.A., 1909.

Hamilton, Angus. Korea. New York: Charles Scribner's Sons, 1904.

Harrington, Fred H. God, Mammon and the Japanese. Madison, Wisc.: University of Wisconsin, 1944.

Hulbert, H. B. "National Examination in Korea," Transactions, Royal Asiatic Society, Vol. XIV, Seoul, 1923.

Kendall, C. W. The Truth About Korea. San Francisco: The Korean National Association, 1919.

BIBLIOGRAPHY

Kennedy, Edgar Sebert. *Mission to Korea*. London: Derek Verschoyle, Ltd., 1952.

Kim, Chong-Pil. *Report to the Council of Bishops*. Seoul, Korea: Methodist News Service, 1960.

Kim, Helen K. "Rural Education for the Regeneration of Korea." Unpublished Ph.D. dissertation, Columbia University, 1931.

Kim, Kyu-Dan. "Rural Church Life." Unpublished manuscript, Seoul, Korea, 1961.

Korean Mission Field, Vol. VII, no. 10, Oct. 1910; Vol. IX, nos. 5-6, May-June, 1908; Vol. XXXIV, no. 5, May 1938.

The Korean Conspiracy Trial: Full Report of the Proceedings . . . Kobe, Japan: Japan Chronicle, 1912-1913. 2v.

Korean Repository, Vol. II, no. 1, Jan. 1895; Vol. II, no. 3, Mar. 1895; Vol. II, no. 5, May 1895; Vol. III, no. 7, July 1896; Vol. V, no. 1, Jan. 1898; Vol. V, no. 7, July 1898.

Korean Review, Mar. 1906.

Korean Survey, Oct. 1955.

McKenzie, F. A. *Korea's Fight for Freedom*. New York: Fleming H. Revell and Co., 1920.

Memorandum on Tuberculosis. Seoul, Korea: Korea National Tuberculosis Association, 1961.

Minutes of the First Annual Meeting of the General Council of the Protestant Evangelical Missions in Korea. Seoul, Korea, 1905.

———— . . . *Second Annual Meeting*. . . . Seoul, Korea, 1906.

———— . . . *Seventh Annual Meeting*. . . . Seoul, Korea, 1911.

Moser, G. "Portuguese Attempts at Opening Korea," *Korean Survey*, Apr. 1955.

Nisbet, Anabel Major. *Day In and Day Out in Korea*. Richmond, Va.: Whittet Press, 1919.

Noble, M. W. *Victorious Lives of Early Christians*. Seoul, Korea: Christian Literature Society, 1933.

Paik, L. George. *The History of Protestant Missions in Korea, 1832-1910*. Pyeng Yang, Korea: Union Christian College Press, 1929.

Paton, Frank H. *Glimpses of Korea, As Seen Through Australian Eyes* . . . Melbourne, Australia: Brown, Prior & Co., [n.d.].

Portway, D. *Korea. Land of the Morning Calm.* London: George C. Harrap, 1953.

Quarto-Centennial Papers. Pyongyang, Korea: Korean Mission of the Presbyterian Church in the U.S.A., 1909.

Report . . . 1961. Seoul, Korea: R. M. Wilson Leprosy Colony, 1961.

Reports of the Joint Deputation to Korea. New York: Korea Committee, Far Eastern Joint Office, F.M.C.N.A., Jan. 9, 1948.

Rhodes, H. A., ed. *History of the Korea Mission, Presbyterian Church, U.S.A., 1884-1934.* Seoul, Korea: Chosen Mission Presbyterian Church U.S.A., 1934.

Rhodes, H. A., ed. *Fiftieth Anniversary Celebration of the Korea Mission of the Presbyterian Church in the U.S.A.* Seoul, Korea: Y.M.C.A. Press, 1934.

Ryang, J. S., ed. *Southern Methodism in Korea, Thirtieth Anniversary.* Seoul, Korea: Board of Missions, Korea Annual Conference Methodist Episcopal Church, South, 1929.

Sauer, C. A., ed. *Within the Gate.* Seoul, Korea: Methodist News Service, 1934.

Smith, John C. "Policy Lessons from Korea," *International Review of Missions,* July, 1961.

Statistical Yearbook, 1960. Seoul, Korea: Republic of Korea, Dept. of Internal Affairs, 1961.

Trollope, Mark N. *The Church in Corea.* London: A. R. Mowbray, 1915.

Underwood, Lillias Horton. *Fifteen Years Among the Top Knots.* New York: American Tract Society, 1904.

Van Buskirk, James Dale. *Korea, Land of the Dawn.* New York: Friendship Press, 1931.

Voelkel, Harold. *Open Door to Korea.* Grand Rapids, Mich.: Zondervan Publishing House, 1958.

Wasson, Alfred Washington. *Church Growth in Korea* (Studies in the World Mission of Christianity. Occasional papers, no. 1) New York: International Missionary Council, 1934.

The Wonderful Story of Christian Missions in Korea; The Results, Conditions and Outlook described by Missionaries and Teachers. (Reprinted from *The Missionary Review of the World*, Feb. and March 1908.) Chicago: Women's Presbyterian Board of Missions of the Northwest, 1908.

Yearbook . . . 1959, 1960-61. Toronto, Canada: United Church of Canada, 1959-61.

PICTURE CREDITS

A WORD ABOUT THE FORMAT

Set in 10 point Electra leaded 3 points
Manufactured by Sowers Printing Company, Lebanon, Pa.
Jackets and paper covers by Affiliated Lithographers, Inc., New York
Text paper, S. D. Warren's #66 Antique

Typographic design and pictorial layout by Margery W. Smith
Binding design by Louise E. Jefferson